A GUIDE-BOOK
TO THE
PRADO MUSEUM

BERNARDINO DE PANTORBA
Member of the Hispanic Society of America, New York

A GUIDE-BOOK
TO THE
PRADO MUSEUM
INCLUDING A COMMENTARY AND
GENERAL HISTORICAL INFORMATION

TRANSLATED INTO ENGLISH BY
CEDRIC SALTER
(B. A. OXON.)

WITH 128 ILLUSTRATIONS

EIGHTH EDITION

COMPAÑIA BIBLIOGRAFICA ESPAÑOLA, S. A.
NIEREMBERG, 14
MADRID

© Compañía Bibliográfica Española, S. A.
Madrid, 1964

NÚM. DE REGISTRO: 3081-50
DEPÓSITO LEGAL. M. 17504.—1964

E. Sánchez Leal, S. A., Dolores, 9, Madrid.

P R E F A C E

The Prado Art Gallery, locally known as the Prado Museum, is undoubtedly the most notable collection of paintings to be found in Spain. With its 2.000 exhibits it is not only the largest collection in terms of quantity, but also the only Spanish picture gallery of international fame. It would not be an exaggeration to say that no cultured visitor to this country willingly fails to visit the Prado, and the Spaniards, in their thousands, reveal their pride in this matchless artistic heritage.

Owing to its great size, and infinitely varied contents, it is essential to employ a guide-book, and we hope that the following pages will meet this need.

The *Guide-Book to the Prado Picture Gallery* has been divided into three separate sections. The first gives information about the Prado of a general character; the second is devoted to a description of the different galleries, together with some comment upon the best-known exhibits, and the third consists of an alphabetic list of the names of the painters whose works are to be seen, and the galleries in which they may be found.

GENERAL INFORMATION
ABOUT THE PRADO

THE PRADO MUSEUM

The Prado Art Gallery is situated in the centre of the city, in the attractive avenue known as the «Paseo del Prado», not far from the famous Plaza de la Cibeles and the Mediodía Railway Station. The luxury Ritz and Palace Hotels, the Jeronimos Church and the Spanish Academy building are all within a few hundred yards. It is also within easy reach of the Spanish Parliament House (Palacio de las Cortes), Bank of Spain, Fine Arts Club and the former Royal Park of the Retiro. The Prado itself faces west, and is fronted by grass lawns and cedar trees, giving it the air of an old palace. In the centre there is a statue of Velázquez.

The south side is also bordered by a small garden and another single statue—that of Murillo. A third—this time of Goya—marks the two entrance doors in the northern front, one on the ground floor and the other reached by a stone stairway leading direct to the first floor, where the best-known paintings are to be found.

The building itself is an attractive example of the neo-classic style, approximately 522 feet in length. The general effect from outside is a harmonious blend of the typical rose-coloured Madrid brick and grey-white Colmenar stone.

It was built towards the end of the XVIIIth. century, during the reign of King Charles IIIrd, according to plans prepared by the Madrid architect Juan de Villanueva. It was intended for a natural science museum, but remained empty for many years. During the War of Independence against Napoleon the building suffered considerable damage, and it was not until 1816 that King Ferdinand VIIth. decided to repair it for use as a picture gallery, at a cost of seven million «reales».

The Prado was opened as a Royal art gallery on the 19th of November, 1819, and it was not until 1868, when Queen Isabella IInd was driven into exile, that it became the property of the nation.

It is supposed that the initiative for the Prado's foundation came from Queen María Isabel de Braganza, the second wife of King Ferdinand VIIth, who was a patroness of the arts, but the Queen died without seeing her plans completed.

In 1819 the Prado contained only 311 paintings, all by Spanish artists, the following among them at that time still being alive, namely, Goya, Vicente López, José Madrazo, José Aparicio, Bartolomé Montalvo and Mariano Sánchez.

The first warden of the Prado, Don Luis Eusebi, produced a simple catalogue, which shows that when it was opened the gallery contained 44 canvases by Velázquez, 44 by Murillo, 43 by the still-life painter Luis Meléndez, 29 by Ribera, 15 by Juan de Juanes, 7 by Alonso Cano, 6 by Zurbarán and 4 by Ribalta. There were only two examples of the work of Goya (who was 73 years old at this time) these being the equestrian portraits of King Charles IVth and Queen María Luisa, both of which are still there today. It is strange to note that there was not a single example of the work of El Greco, and only one canvas by an artist belonging to his school. This is partly accounted for by the fact that in those days El Greco did not enjoy the tremendous reputation he possesses today, and was in any case considered an Italian, rather than a Spanish, painter. Strange though it may seem to us it is only 150 years since Greco was described as «insane»!

This original catalogue contained paintings which were already famous, such as *Las Meninas*, *The Spinners*, *The Topers*, *The Surrender of Breda*, *The Forge of Vulcan*, *The Holy Family «del Pajarito»*, Murillo's *Madonnas*; *Saint Bartholomew's Martyrdom*, by Ribera; *The Last Supper*, by Juan de Juanes, and *Saint Casilda*, by Zurbarán.

The entire original collection of 311 paintings was hung in three galleries on the first floor.

During the year 1821, 195 works by Italian painters were added, including canvases by Titian, Raphael, Tintoretto, Veronese, Guercino, Bassano, Guido Reni, Andrea del Sarto, Mantegna, Bellini, Sebastiano del Piombo, Lucca Giordano and, in 1843, the first examples of Rubens and Van Dyck.

The palaces of the Spanish Royal family at the beginning of the XIXth. century contained no less than 5.539 paintings, and the Prado received a considerable number of these during the next 70 years. In addition it obtained valuable legacies from the Museo Nacional de la Trinidad in 1870; from Count Emil d'Erlanger in 1881; Don Ramón de Errazu in 1904; the Duchess of Villahermosa in 1905; Don Pablo Bosch in 1915; Don Pedro Fernández-Durán in 1930, and Don Francisco Cambó in 1941. It is a remarkable fact that there has never been a disputed title of ownership regarding any picture on exhibition in the Prado, nor any case of fire or robbery, though some jewels were stolen from the Tesoro del Delfin in 1918. There is a special studio on the ground floor, permanently at the disposal of a group of artist experts for the painstaking restoration of damaged canvases.

There is an official catalogue signed by the Director of the Prado, Don Francisco Xavier Sánchez Cantón, which contains a brief and accurate list of all the paintings on exhibition.

Although the fame of the Prado is founded upon its collection of paintings it also contains many fine sculptures, over 300 of them, all of marble or bronze, being distributed throughout the different galleries. On the ground floor are the jewelry exhibits known as the *Tesoro del Delfin.*

The space available for the magnificent collection of drawings is totally inadequate, and only about one sixth of them are on exhibition on the second floor, including no less than 470 from the hand of Goya. Additionally, the Prado contains a remarkable collection of furniture, tapestry, weapons, ceramics and porcelain, embroideries, miniatures, coins and medals—most of them being legacies from private benefactors.

Of the three thousand paintings possessed by the Prado the 2.283 best are on view there, the others being on loan to provincial art galleries and Government offices. This figure is made up as follows; 835 by Spanish painters, 661 by Flemish, 435 by Italian, 157 by French, 138 by Dutch, 43 by German, 9 by English and 3 by Swedish masters. There are also two other paintings on exhibition, one by a Portuguese and the other by an artist of unknown nationality.

A resume of the subject matter shows that, in this total, 870 are on religious themes, from the Old and New Testament or scenes from the lives of the Saints; 478 portraits; 150 mythological paintings; 172 landscapes and seascapes, 120 studies of flowers and still life, 50 on historical subjects and 443 interiors, allegorical, etc.

The majority of the works on show in the Prado are oil paintings, but there are also frescos; a ceiling decorated by Vicente López; some Spanish and Italian primitives; a few paintings in «gouache» by Pedro Berruguete, some wall frescos by Antoniazzo Romano, Antonio Mohedano and Melozzo da Forli, and some water-colours by Mariano Fortuny and Martín Rico.

The latest catalogue of the Prado shows that some 500 painters have examples of their work on view, of which 120 are Spanish, 120 Italian, over 100 Flemish, some 50 Dutch, 40 French, 10 German and 7 English.

In alphabetical order the Prado includes works by the Spanish painters Benito Manuel de Agüero, Francisco and José Antolínez, Juan de Arellano, Antonio Arias, Francisco and Ramón Bayeu, Gaspar Becerra, Bartolomé Bermejo, Pedro Berruguete, Pedro Atanasio Bocanegra, Juan Martín Cabezalero, Francisco Camilo, Alonso Cano, Vicencio Carducho, Antonio Carnicero, Juan Carreño de Miranda, Antonio del Castillo, Eugenio Caxés, Mateo Cerezo, Claudio Coello, Francisco Collantes, Juan Correa, Juan Antonio Escalante, Jerónimo Jacinto Espinosa, Juan de Espinosa, Antonio María Esquivel, Agustín Esteve, Jerónimo Antonio de Ezquerra, Alejo Fernández, Joaquín Manuel Fernández Cruzado, Gregorio Ferro, Mariano Fortuny, Fernando Gallego, Pedro García de Benabarre, Mateo Gilarte, Jacinto Gómez Pastor, Bartolomé González, Zacarías González Velázquez, Francisco Goya, el Greco, Juan Van der Hamen, Francisco de Herrera *el Viejo*, and *el Mozo*, Jaume Huguet, Joaquín Inza, Ignacio Iriarte, José Jiménez Donoso, Juan de Juanes, Fray Joaquín Juncosa, Jusepe Leonardo, Vicente López Portaña, Bernardo López Piquer, Pedro Machuca, José, Federico and Raimundo de Madrazo, Mariano Salvador Maella, Fray Juan Bautista Maino, Esteban March, Vicente Juan Masip, Juan Bautista Martínez del Mazo, Luis Eugenio and Miguel Jacinto Meléndez,

Antonio Mohedano, Luis de Morales, Sebastián Muñoz, Bartolomé
Esteban Murillo, Juan Fernández Navarrete *el Mudo*, Pedro de
Orrente, Francisco Pacheco, Acisclo Antonio de Palomino, Juan
Pantoja de la Cruz, Juan de Pareja, Luis Paret, Antonio de Pere-
da, Bartolomé Pérez, Blas del Prado, Antonio Puga, Felipe Ramí-
rez, Francisco Ribalta, José Ribelles, José de Ribera, Martín Rico,
Fernando del Rincón, Francisco and Fray Juan Rizi, Pedro Ruiz
González, Francisco Salmerón, Alonso Sánchez Coello, Cornelio
Schut *el Mozo*, Juan de Sevilla, Jorge Manuel Theotocopuli, Alonso
Miguel de Tobar, Juan de Toledo, Luis Tristán, Juan de Valdés
Leal, Diego Velázquez, Pedro Antonio Vidal, Antonio Viladomat,
Pedro de Villafranca, Rodrigo de Villandrando, Pedro Núñez de
Villavicencio, Miguel Ximénez, Hernando Yáñez de la Almedina,
Ignacio Zuloaga and Francisco de Zurbarán.

There are also a number of Spanish painters who are known
only as the Masters of Sigüenza, Sisla (Castilian), Arguis (Aragonese), Estimariu (Catalan) Perea (Valencian), Archbishop Dalmau
de Mur (Aragonese), Robledo (native of Burgos), of the Eleven
Thousand Virgins (native of Segovia) and Master of Saint Nicholas (native of Burgos). There are also works by Jorge Ingles and
Nicholas Frances.

The different schools which together constitute the best examples of Italian art, are also represented in the Prado, the Venetian
being predominant. There are also works from the Florentine, Roman, Bolognese, Neapolitan, Lombard and Ferrarese schools of
painting.

There is a fine, though smaller, collection of Flemish, Dutch,
German and French painters, which give an excellent over-all impression of European art as a whole, though the English painters
are rather inadequately represented.

There is a good collection of Flemish «primitives» (XIVth. and
XVth. centuries) but only a limited number by early Italian and
Spanish masters. In general, the large collection of Spanish paintings dates from the XVIth. and XVIIth. centuries leading up to
the very complete representation of the genius of Goya.

The greatest number of canvases exhibited in the Prado by
any individual artist are the 115 oil paintings and 470 crayon or
charcoal drawings by Goya. Next come Velázquez and Ribera,
both with 50, Murillo with 40, Greco with 34, Zurbarán with 22,

Juan de Juanes with 12, Carreño with 11, Sánchez Coello with 10, Claudio Coello with 9, Morales with 8, Pantoja with 8, Alonso Cano with 9, Mazo with 8, Pereda with 6, Valdés Leal, Tristán, Ribalta and Maino with 4.

Titian is the best represented of the Italian artists, with 36 authenticated works, while Lucca Giordano has 29, Tintoretto 26, Veronese 15, Corrado Giaquinto 10, Tiepolo 10 and Raphael 8.

Other Italian painters exhibited at the Prado are: Francesco Albani, Alessandro and Cristofano Allori, Jacopo Amiconi, Fra Angelico, Lucia Anguisciola, Antoniazzo Romano, Antonio Badile, Barocci, the three Bassanos (Francesco, Jacopo and Leandro), Pompeo Girolamo Battoni, Giovanni Bellini, Andrea Belvedere, Giovanni Biliverti, Giuseppe Bonito, Pietro Bonzi, Paris Bordone, Orazio Borgiani, Sandro Botticelli, Il Bronzino, Antonio and Vicencio Campi, Il Canaletto, Lucca Cangiaso, Giovanni Battista Caracciolo, Bartolomé Carducci, Girolamo da Carpi, Agostino and Annibale Carracci, Giovanni Castiglione, Il Catena, Giacomo Cavedone, Giovanni Bettino Cignaroli, Cima da Conegliano, Viviano Codazzi, Sebastiano Conca, Il Correggio, Pietro da Cortona, Danielle and Giovanni Battista Crespi, Il Domenichino, Dosso Dossi, Gasparo Dughet, Aniello Falcone, Cesare Fracanzano, Giacomo and Giulio Francia, Francesco Furini, Taddeo Gaddi, Filippo Gagliardi, Artemisa and Orazio Gentileschi, Gian Francesco Gessi, Il Giorgione, Il Guercino, Antonio Joli, Giovanni di Stéfano Lanfranco, Bernardino Licinio, Lorenzo Lotto, Bernardino Luini, Maineri da Parma, Pietro Malombra, Rutilio di Lorenzo Manetti, Bartolommeo Manfredi, Andrea Mantegna, Carlo Maratti, Melozzo da Forli, Giovanni Battista Moroni, Jacopo Nani, Giuseppe Nogari, Pietro Novelli, Il Padovanino, the two Palmas (*Elder* and *Younger*), Giovanni Paolo Panini, Il Parmigianino, Michele Parrasio, Perino del Vaga, Gianbattista Piazzetta, Marco dal Pino, Sebastiano del Piombo, Giovanni dal Ponte, Il Pontormo, Carlo Portelli, Mattia Preti, Andrea and Camilo Procaccini, Domenico Puligo, Guido Reni, Giulio Romano, Salvatore Rosa, Francesco Rossi, Andrea Sacchi, Domenico Sani, Andrea del Sarto, Il Sassoferrato, Francesco Solimena, Lionello Spada, Massimo Stanzione, Bernardo Strozzi, Giovanni Domenico Tiepolo, Marietta Robusti (*the Tintoretta*), Domenico Tintoretto, Alessandro Turchi, Andrea

Cristo presentado al pueblo.   Jesus shown to the people.
Le Christ présenté au peuple.   Christus wird vor das Volk geführt.

La Visitación.   The Visitation.
La Visitation.   Die Heimsuchung Marias.

Santa Bárbara (fragmento).   Saint Barbara (detail).
Sainte Barbe (détail).   Heilige Barbara (fragment).

VAN DER WEYDEN

El Descendimiento de la Cruz.
La Descente de la Croix.

The Descent from the Cross.
Die Kreuzabnahme.

HANS MEMLING

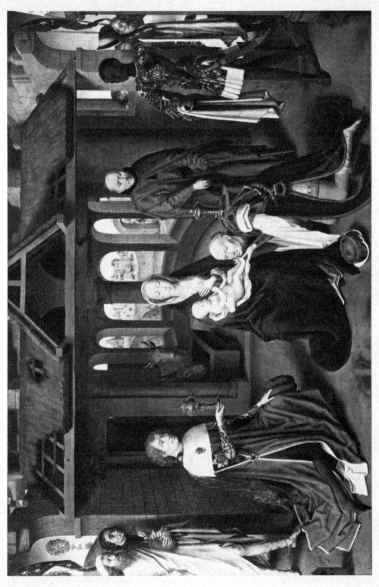

La Epifanía (centro del tríptico).
L'Epiphanie.

The Epiphany.
Dreikönigstag.

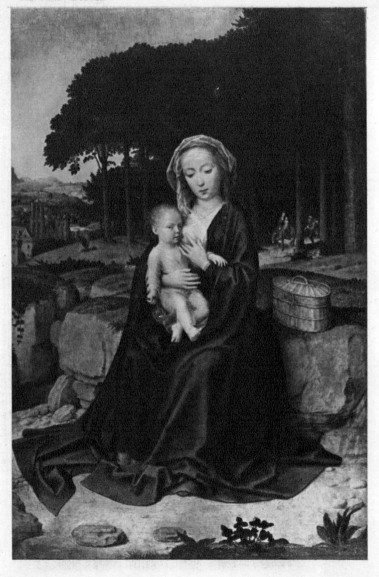

Descanso en la Huída a Egipto.   The Rest during the Flight into Egypt.
Le Repos dans la Fuite en Egypte.   Rast auf der Flucht nach Aegypten.

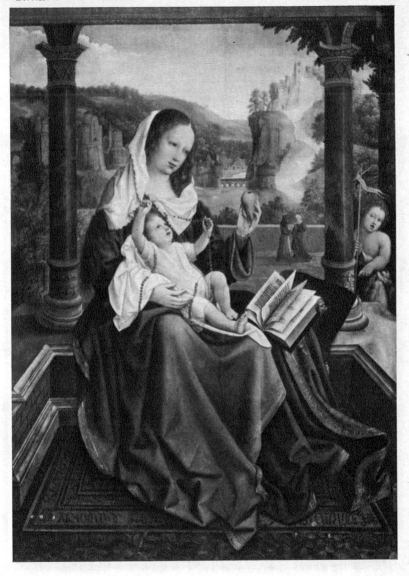

La Virgen con el Niño.　　　　Virgin and Child.
La Vierge avec l'Enfant.　　　Maria mit dem Kinde.

PATINIR

Paisaje con San Jerónimo.
Paysage avec Saint Jérôme.

Landscape with St. Jerome.
Landschaft mit St. Jeronimus.

PEETER BRUEGHEL

El Triunfo de la Muerte.
Le Triomphe de la Mort.

The Triumph of Death.
Der Sieg des Todes.

HIERONYMUS BOSCH

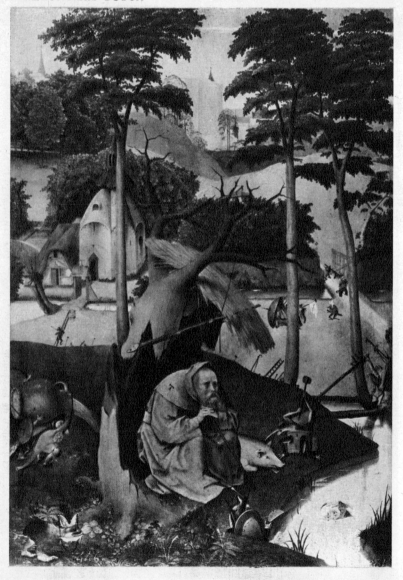

Las tentaciones de S. Antonio.   The Temptations of St. Anthony.
Les tentations de Saint Antoine.   Die Versuchungen des Heil. Antonius.

El carro de heno (tabla central).   The Chaff cart (centre).
Le chariot de foin (panneau principal).   Der Heuwagen (haupttafel).

HIERONYMUS BOSCH

El Jardin de las Delicias (fragmento).   The Garden of Pleasure (detail).
Le Jardin des Délices (détail).   Der Garten des Genusses (fragment).

VAN HEMESEN

El cirujano.   The Surgeon.
Le chirurgien.   Der Chirurg.

Autorretrato.   Self-portrait.
Portrait de l'auteur.   Selbstbildnis.

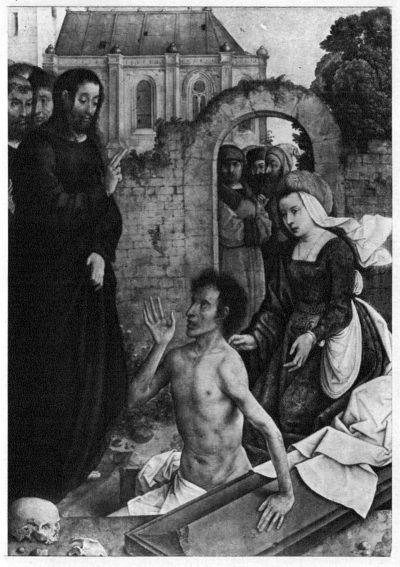

La Resurrección de Lázaro.
La Résurrection de Lazare.

The Resurrection of Lazarus.
Die Auferweckung des Lazarus.

Auto de fe.

Vaccaro, Carlo Veronese, Gaspar van Vitelli, Danielle da Volterra and Battista Zelotti.

Among Flemish painters Rubens is the best represented in the Prado, there being more than 80 examples of his work on exhibition, if you include a certain number done in collaboration with other painters of his school. Then comes Jan Brueghel de Velours, with 40, David Teniers (Son) with 39, Anton van Dyck, with 25 and Frans Snyders, with 22.

Other Flemish painters include: Alexander van Adriaensen, Denis van Alsloot, Jacques d'Arthois, Osias Beet, Ambrosius Benson, Jacob Andries Beschey, Jan Frans and Peeter van Bloemen, Peter Boel, Jean Baptiste Borkens, Andries Bosmans, Adriaan Frans Boudewyms, Peter Bout, Thierry Bouts, Paul Brill, Adriaen Brouwer, Peeter Brueghel *Elder*, Brueghel *Younger*, Jan de Cock, Pieter Coecke, Marcellus Coffermans, Alexander Coosemans, Jan Cossiers, Adam de Coster, Michel Coxcie, Joost van Craesbeeck, Gaspar de Crayer, Petrus Christus, Cornelis van Dalem, Gerard David, Jacob Fopens van Es, Gaspard van Eyck, Jan Eyck, John of Flandes, Frans Francken *(Elder, Younger* and the son of the latter), Jan Fyt, Antoon Gunther Ghering, Jacob Peter Gowi, Jan Sanders van Hemesen, Peeter Huys, Adriaen Isenbrandt, Jacob Jordaens, Jan van Kessel *(Elder* and *Younger)*, Christoph van der Lamen, Pietro de Lignis, Lambert Lombard, Frans Luyck, Christiaan Luycks, *Jan de Mabuse,* Jan Massys, Quentin Metsys, Hans Memling, Adan van der Meulen, Peeter Meuleneur, Theobald Michau, Jan van Bike Miel, Anton Mirou, Peeter van Mol, Josse de Momper, Ludwig Neefs, Peter Neefs *(the Elder),* Nicholas of Neufchatel, Bernard van Orley, Joachim Patinir, Bonaventura Peeters, Clara Peeters, Frans Pourbus *(the Younger)*, Jan Prevost, Erasmus Quellyn, Jan Reyn, Theodor Rombouts, David Ryckaert, Daniel Seghers, Gerard Seghers, Peeter Snayers, Joris van Son, Adriaen van Stalbent, Ignatius van der Stock, Mathaus Stomer, Justus Susterman, Peeters Symons, Abraham and David Teniers, Jan Philips van Thielen, Justus Tiel, Theodore van Tulden, Lukas van Uden, Adriaen van Utrecht, Lukas van Valckenborgh, Cornelis and Paul de Vos, Roger van der Weyden, Jan Wildens, Artus Wolfordt, Catherine Ykens and Frans Ykens.

Of the French painters, Jean Ranc, Nicolas Poussin and Claude de Lorraine, with 14, 12 and 10 works respectively are the best represented in the Prado. Other French painters, whose works are listed, are: Paul Baudry, Charles and Henri Beaubrun, Jean de Boullogne, Sebastien Bourdon, Antoine François Callet, Courtilleau, Jacques Courtois, Antoine Coypel, Philippe de Champaigne, Michel Dorigny, François Hubert Drouais, Domenico Dupra, Joseph Bernat Flaugier, Charles Joseph Flipart, Charles de la Fósse, Pierre Gobert, Jean Baptiste Greuze, Michel-Ange Houasse, Charles François Hutin, Jean Baptiste Jouvenet, Louis Jean François Lagrenée, Nicolas Largillière, Louis Michel van Loo, Joseph Laurent Malaine, Jean Louis Ernest Meissonier, Pierre Mignard, Jean Marc Nattier, Jean Nocret, Jean Baptiste Oudry, Jean Pillement, François Pret, Hyacinthe Rigaud, Hubert Robert, Louis Silvestre, Charles François de la Traverse, Claude Joseph Vernet, Simon Vouet and Jean Antoine Watteau.

Dutch painters include Anthony Moro with 15 works. Then come Philips Wouverman, with 11; and Bosch, with 8. Other Dutch painters represented here are: Adriaen Backer, Jacob Adriaensz Bellevois, Adriaen Bloemaert, Andries and Johannes Both, Leonard Bramer, Quiringh Gerritsz van Brekelencam, Pieter Claeszon, David Colyn, Coosemas, Adriaen Cronenburch, Joost Cornelisz Droochsloot, Hendrick Jacobsz Dubbels, Pieter Fris, Jan Glauber (named Polidoro), Pieter Grebber, Cornelis van Harlem, Willem Klaesz Heda, Jan Davidsz de Heem, Lucas de Heere, Meindert Hobbema, Gerard van Honthorst, Cornelis Johnson, Jan Kraek, Gabriel Metsu, Michiel Janszoón van Mierevelt, Hendrick van Minderhout, Eglon Hendrick van der Neer, Pieter Nolpe, Jacob Cornelisz van Oostsanen, Adriaen van Ostade, Anthonie Palamedes, Gerard Jan Palthe, Johannes Parcellis, Cornelis van Poelenburg, Paulus Potter, Rembrandt, Marinus Claeszon van Reymerswaele, Jacob Isacksz van Ruysdael, T. Sauts, Jan van Scorel, Godfried Schalcken, Johannes Pietersz Schoeff, Hendrick van Steenwijk (the Younger), Pieter Steenwijck, Hermann van Swanevelt, Joachim Antonisz Uytewael, Hermann van Vollenhoven and Cornelis Claesz van Wiringen.

German painting is represented in the Prado by Anton Raphael Mengs, with 22 works; Albrecht Dürer with 4; and other painters such as Christoph Amberger, Hans Baldung, Lucas Cranach (the Elder), Adam Elsheimer, Angelica Kauffmann, Israhel von Meckenen, Philipp Peter Roos and Jan Christian Vollardt.

David Roberts, John Hoppner, Joshua Reynolds, Thomas Gainsborough, John Waston Gordon, Thomas Lawrence and George Romney, are the only English painters whose work may be seen in the Prado.

Additionally there are the Swedish painters Adolf Ulrik Wertmüller and Anders Zorn, the Portuguese Domingo Carvalho and the painter J. P. de Lioutherbbourg of unknown nationality. There are also over 200 paintings by anonymous artists.

The outstanding painters not represented in the Prado are the Van Eyck Brothers, van der Goes, Lucas de Leyden, Vermeer de Delft, Frans Hals, Leonardo de Vinci, Il Caravaggio, Il Perugino, Holbein, Grünewald, Fragonard, Le Brun and Nuño Gonsalves, and there are also very few examples of the Italian fresco painters of the XVth. century.

Very great care has been taken to establish the authenticity of every picture exhibited in the Prado and, whenever there is any doubt on the subject, they are listed as anonymous works by pupils of the school of this or that master. No one, for example, would be prepared to guarantee that the pictures named *The Fount of Grace, Portrait of an Old Man* and *La Gioconda* are not the works of the Van Eyck Brothers, of Holbein and Leonardo, respectively, but they are not exhibited as being by these Masters, as all elements of doubt as to their authorship cannot be removed. The *Gioconda* in the possession of the Prado is in no way inferior to the famous one in the Louvre, and the *Portrait of an Old Man* is as good as any of Holbein's work, while the *Fount of Grace* is equally impressive when compared with the authenticated work of the great Flemish painter.

The Prado at present contains 116 numbered galleries or halls, 42 on the ground floor, 53 on the first floor and 21 on the top floor.

In the first floor are gathered the most outstanding masterpieces of the whole Prado collection: Velázquez, Goya, el Greco, Murillo, Ribera, Zurbarán, Titian, Raphael, Tintoretto, Veronese, Bassanos, Rubens, Van Dyck and Jordaens. Here, too, are the best Flemish primitives, including panels by Dürer, and Botticelli, and others by Fra Angelico and Mantegna.

No attempt can be made to estimate the monetary value of the Prado collection. In 1834, at the death of King Ferdinand VIIth. such an attempt was made in order to divide it between his two daughters, Isabella and Luisa Fernanda. However, as the object of the valuers was to ensure that the best pictures remained in the hands of the Monarch, the estimate was intentionally low in order to enable Isabella to buy out her younger sister inexpensively. As a result their figure of 30 ½ million «reales» gives us no clear idea of its true value. In any case, in the 127 years since then, the market value of pictures has increased an hundred-fold, and the sale value of the collection remains incalculable.

TOUR OF THE MUSEUM

ROTUNDA

Upon entering the Prado by the staircase leading direct to the first floor there is a large circular hall, dominated by a bronze group by Leone and Pompeo Leoni, of Charles Vth. At his feet there is a recumbent figure, symbolic of the Emperor's triumphs over his enemies. This is a fine example of Renaissance sculpture, and is dated 1564. It is notable for the fact that the magnificent armour worn by the Emperor can be removed, revealing a naked body worthy of a Greek hero.

On the walls of this circular hall six of the twelve pictures, ordered by King Philip IVth. to decorate the Salón de Reinos in his Palace of the Buen Retiro, are on exhibition. These depict various Spanish victories of the period, three of them by an Italian painter who adopted Spanish nationality, Vicente Carducho; two by Eugenio Caxes, and one by the Aragonese painter Jusepe Leonardo. The remaining three, which are the best, are *The Surrender of Breda*, by Velázquez; *The Recapture of Bahia*, by Father Maino, and *The Relief of Genoa*, by Pereda. These pictures, which suffer from poor lighting, are chiefly of interest as the forerunners of the historical painting to which various Spanish masters devoted themselves during the XIXth. century.

FLEMISH AND GERMAN PRIMITIVES

To the right of this circular hall there is a small door leading to a series of five galleries numbered XL, XLI, XLII, XLIII and XLIV, devoted to the exhibition of early Flemish and German paintings. There are over seventy examples, against

a background of ochre coloured tapestry. In the first gallery
there are works by Quentin Metsys, Van der Weyden, Gossaert,
Thierry Bouts, Petrus Christus, Isenbrandt and the so-called
Masters of Flémalle, of the Divine Blood and Hoogstraten. In
the second, Van der Weyden and Memling are represented,
together with a number of less notable pieces by Van Orley,
Juan de Flandes and Jean de Cock. The third contains further
Isenbrandts, Van Orleys, Gossaerts. Pieter Coeckes and Gerard
Davids, as well as the Master of Francfort and the Divine
Blood. In the fourth, there are works by Patinir, Brueghel
(the Elder) and Bosch. The last gallery contains examples of Albrecht Dürer, Hans Baldung, Lucas Granach, Van Reymerswaele, Bosch, Isenbrandt, Israhel van Meckenen, Sanders van
Hemesen and a possible Holbein. The collection is completed
by a number of anonymous works from the Flemish school.

This collection of early XVth. century paintings reveals the mastery achieved in Northern Europe at that period, and lacks only
examples of the work of Jan Van Eyck and Van der Goes (1) to
be among the most complete in Europe.

The belief that Huberto and Jan Van Eyck were the originators
of oil painting on wooden panels is not undisputed, but there
is no doubt that their superb technique was responsible for the
acceptance of the use of oils in painting throughout Europe. Their
contribution to Art is all the more remarkable as, in their short
lives, the brothers Van Eyck not only introduced a new technique
but themselves achieved a mastery of it that was never subsequently surpassed. This is emphasised not only by the intense vitality
of the works themselves, but also by the extraordinary purity of
colour and subtlety of tone that have triumphantly survived the
passage of over five centuries. Their precision in representing the
design and texture of materials is unequalled in its beauty and
restraint. The host of imitators that followed during the succeeding
centuries never achieved the same astonishing blend of painstaking
workmanship and inspired genius.

------

(1)   King Philip IInd. was the owner of one of the finest of all Van Eyck's
paintings, known as *The Arnolfini Marriage* but, during the Peninsular War
against Napoleon, it was sent to England. where it is today on exhibition in
the National Gallery. *The Epiphany*, by Van der Goes, was also the property
of the Colegio de Monforte de Lemos until early in the present century but,
owing to the indifference of the authorities, it was sold to the Berlin Museum
for the sum of 1.268.800 pesetas.

However, before the Flemish School finally lost the inspiration of its founders, there were many worthy disciples of the Van Eyck brothers who carried on their tradition. Among these were Roger van der Weyden, Hans Memling, Thierry Bouts, and Petrus Christus. Early in the XVIth. century they were succeeded by Gerard David, Quentin Metsys, Jan Gossaert, Joachim Patinir, Adriaen Isenbrandt, Barend van Orley, Jan Sanders van Hemesen, Pieter Coecke van Aels, Hyeronimus van Aeken and Marinus Claeszon van Reymerswaele, Brueghel belongs to a later generation. In the following pages we will briefly examine their works.

HALL XL

There are five outstanding paintings in this room. They are *Christ shown to the people*, by Metsys; *Christ with the Virgin Mary and John the Baptist*, by Gossaert; *St. Barbara* and *The Betrothal of the Virgin*, by the Master of Flémalle, and *The Fount of Grace*, ascribed to the school of the Van Eyck brothers.

Christ shown to the people, by Metsys. This picture was in the collection of the Marqués de Remisa until it was left, as a legacy to the Prado, by Don Mariano Lanuza, in 1940. The first impression is that, despite the size of the panel and the fine colouring, the figures suffer from crowding. However, a vivid contrast is achieved between the serene figure of Christ and the cruel and mocking faces of his executioners, and the robes of a bearded Jew make a satisfying splash of warm red in the foreground.

Christ with the Virgin Mary & St. John the Baptist, by Gossaert. This picture was in the Escorial Monastery until 1839, and it was only then that its authorship was finally established. The influence of the Van Eycks is marked, and the treatment of the adolescent Mary and the rustic figure of St. John the Baptist are strongly reminiscent of the famous Van Eyck *Adoration of the Mystic Lamb.*

The Fount of Grace (Van Eyck School). This is an allegorical representation of the triumph of Christianity over Judaism, as revealed in a vision of St. Hildegard. The diversity of detail in the background, both human and architectural, shows the same extraordinary mastery of composition which is the unmistakable hallmark of the genuine Flemish primitive. The three main figures, and choirs of singing angels, are grouped round the Lamb in the upper part of the picture. Below is the Fount of Grace, upon the waters of which is floating the Eucharist. To one side are the figures of Christians, and on the other a group of Jews, blindly turning away from the Waters of Life.

This picture was known to be in the Monastery of El Parral in Segovia in 1454, and then belonged to the collection of the Museo de la Trinidad until its removal to the Prado in 1827. During the whole of its stay in the Museo de la Trinidad it was officially ascribed to Jan van Eyck. who was believed to have visited Spain in 1428.

Before leaving this room we advise any visitor to glance at the poliptych known as *The Visitation.* Perhaps the most beautiful of the panels is that representing *The Epiphany*, which was first ascribed to Petrus Christus, but is now attributed to Bouts. This also came to the Prado from the Escorial in 1839.

St. Barbara, by the Master of Flémalle: This is a delicate study of an interior. St. Barbara is represented as a typical Flemish woman, placidly reading her prayer-book, against a domestic background of homely furniture. It was painted in 1438, bought by King Charles IVth, and came to the Prado from the Royal Palace at Aranjuez in 1827.

The Betrothal of the Virgin, by the Master of Flémalle. For some unknown reason art critics have not given this work its due, although it will bear comparison with the best work of the XVth. century Flemish Masters. It was brought from El Escorial in 1839. The figures of St. James the Apostle and St. Clara on the outer leaves of the triptych have suggested to some experts that the painter known as «the Master of Flémalle» may have been Robert Campin, the teacher of van der Weyden, or even that he may have been van der Weyden himself.

HALL XLI

This room is devoted to the works of Van der Weyden and Memling.

The Descent from the Cross, by Van der Weyden was painted in 1435 for the Chapel of Our Lady of Victory in Louvain. A century later it was sold to Queen Mary of Hungary, Governor of the Low Countries, in exchange for a new organ for the Church, its value being represented as 500 florins, though the Queen also undertook to fill the space formerly occupied by the picture with an exact copy by Michel Coxcie.

Van der Weyden's picture was then sent to King Philip IInd, nephew of Queen Mary, but the ship in which it was being transported was wrecked, and the case in which it had been packed was only recovered with great difficulty. Philip IInd. presented it to El Escorial, where it remained for over three and a half centuries, when it replaced another copy by Coxcie already in the Prado.

The Descent from the Cross contains ten figures on a golden background, and an observer is immediately struck by the dramatic quality of the composition, which marks Van der Weyden's work with a deeper religious and emotional appeal than that of any of his contemporaries. Surrounded by the placid and innocent representations of the Virgin and Child so typical of the Flemish school, *The Descent* strikes an authentic note of high tragedy. Despite the characteristic rigidity and exact drawing of Christ's body and His Mother's hands, the whole picture is vital with life and feeling, and the two weeping female figures still further emphasise the sense of drama. It is, perhaps, of interest to observe that the painter had to extend the original panel in order to include the Cross and the male figure on the ladder helping to lower the dead Christ.

Beside *The Descent* there is a small panel named *Piety* which is notable for its modern-seeming brilliance of colour, though the theme is still the tragic one of the Virgin laying her tearful face against that of her dead Son. This work of the artist known as Master Roger was bought by the Prado from the Duke of Mandas in 1925. There is a much inferior duplicate in the Berlin Museum.

The great triptych *The Redemption* was the property of the Madrid Convent of Los Angeles, founded by Doña Leonor Mascareñas, one-time nurse to King Philip IInd. From there it passed to the Museo de la Trinidad, and finally to the Prado, though doubts have occasionally been raised as to whether it is an authentic Van der Weyden.

The centre panel of the triptych depicts Christ on the Cross between the Virgin Mary and St. John, with a Gothic church in the background. The left-hand panel shows the Expulsion from Eden, and that on the right represents the Last Judgment.

The centre panel is unquestionably the best, Van der Weyden's occasional tendency to over-emphasise facial expression being kept within limits and, by studying it, we can understand how his work came to exercise a greater influence on Spanish Art during the late XVth. and early XVIth. century than that of any other painter of the Flemish primitive school.

Reinach has written that the work of Hans Memling—sometimes called the Raphael of Flemish Art—is the most original and attractive of the Flemish school. His triptych known as *The Epiphany* was the property of the Emperor Charles Vth, and was in the oratory of Ateca Castle until it was brought to the Prado in 1847. According to some experts it was painted in 1470, and there is another original by the same artist in the Bruges Hospital, signed and dated 1479.

The central panel possesses a serene beauty, and the whole triptych reveals the richness of colour and intricate exactness of design and drawing characteristic of the Flemish school, while the facial expressions reveal a profound study in character.

HALL XLII

The outstanding pictures in this room are *The Virgin of Louvain*, by Gossaert; *Virgin and Child*, by Van Orley; *The Mass of St. Gregory*, by Isenbrandt, and *The Rest during the Flight into Egypt*, by Gerard David, this last providing strong evidence that

David was probably the best Flemish painter of the XVth. century, and worthy heir to Memling.

David's panel is undoubtedly the best of the three in the Prado ascribed to him, and the fine brushwork used to depict every detail of the background is beyond praise. Incidentally, another identical original is in the possession of a British Gallery.

Doubts have been raised as to whether or not the *Virgin of Louvain* is the work of Gossaert, as it differs considerably from his usual style, and some experts ascribe it to Van Orley. Painted in 1516 it came to the Prado from El Escorial in 1839.

HALLS XLIII AND XLIV

The outstanding figure, marking the transition of the Flemish School from the XVth. to the XVIth. century, is the landscape painter Patinir, and his work is immediately recognisable for the unusual green tones which he employed to achieve a strangely dreamlike quality. The human figures only serve as an explanation of the title of *The Flight into Egypt,* and it is the unearthly light shining upon the background which arrests and holds our interest.

The Passage of the Styx is another magnificent example of the work of Patinir, ranking with *The Rest on the Flight into Egypt.* These two pictures, together with his signed *St. Jerome,* showing the Saint in the midst of another unmistakable Patinir landscape, also came to the Prado from El Escorial. *The Temptations of St. Anthony* was made in collaboration with Quentin Metsys, who painted the figures.

All visitors are instantly arrested by the extraordinary nightmare quality of Brueghel's *Triumph of Death.* The whole conception is infused with a profound sense of tragedy, and the brilliant use of greys and greens make it one of the most remarkable pictures in the whole collection. It came to the Prado from the Palace of San Ildefonso in 1827, and is believed to have been painted in 1560 when Brueghel was at the height of his creative powers.

Peeter Brueghel died before he was fifty, so that there are not a great number of his works in existence, and there are only some 30 examples to be seen from the short period of ten years that he devoted to painting. Pleasure-loving, and content with the placid life that surrounded him, *The Triumph of Death* reveals an unexpected aspect of his character.

There is reason to suppose that Jerome van Aeken lived in Spain for a number of years when, finding his Dutch name of Hieronymus Bosch too difficult, the Spaniards referred to him as *el Bosco*.

He was one of the favourite artists of King Philip IInd. as a result of which there are several of his best works still in El Escorial, in addition to the seven bequeathed to the Prado. Probably one of the principal reasons why his works appealed so greatly to Philip IInd—himself something of a visionary, who latterly revealed symptoms of religious mania—was the artist's predilection for religious themes and visions fully understandable only to a psycho-analyst.

Although Friedländer expresses the opinion that the triptych *The Adoration of the Magi* is «the best thing painted by El Bosco», others consider *The Garden of Pleasure, The Chaff Cart* and *The Deadly Sins* better examples of the artist's extraordinary technique.

The Chaff Cart is a triptych suggested by one of the Psalms. The centre panel represents the pleasures of the senses, pursued by those forgetful of the warning that their enjoyment «flieth like chaff before the winds». In one corner of the picture there is a representation of Paradise, showing the creation of Eve, the Temptation and the Fall. In the opposite corner Hell is shown and, when closed, the triptych as a whole represents *The Path of Life.* This masterpiece was bought by Queen Isabel IInd. in 1848 from Don José de Salamanca for 16.000 «reales».

The Garden of Pleasure is also in the form of a triptych, and came to the Prado from El Escorial only a few years ago. It was bought by King Philip IInd. at an auction of the property of an illegitimate son of the great Duke of Alba in 1592.

The main panel shows a strange grouping of human figures together with animals, birds and fish, which are presumably an allegorical representation of sensuality. The left panel shows the

Creation of the World, while Hell is depicted on the opposite panel. When the two leaves are closed it reveals another representation of the Creation, and the flowering of the first trees and plants.

It is difficult to find a suitable title for this triptych, which is usually referred to by the Spaniards as *The Garden of Licence*, or *The Wages of Sin*. The scene is of a wild glade in some tropical Garden of Eden, peopled by naked human figures and strange animals. It is not difficult to see the influence of the recently reported discovery of America upon the artist's imagination, at a time when Christopher Columbus himself was convinced that he had discovered the Garden of Eden near the mouth of the River Orinoco.

In the left panel's picture of Paradise, where the newly-created Eve is revealed to Adam, all the tropical animals, real and imaginary, known to the Middle Ages are represented. Elephant, giraffe and unicorn; flying--fish, giant saurians and birds with three heads, all disport themselves against a background of trees, symbolic of love.

The central panel depicts a thickly wooded glade. Through the branches of this there is a glimpse of a shining lake, along the banks of which there is a procession of human figures, riding astride upon panthers, horses, deer, wolves, lions, camels, bears, griffins, unicorns and boar, followed by the witch-like figure of a Nature-Priestess. The foreground of the panel is occupied by the shapes of vast imaginary tropical plants.

The artist obviously wished to convey the message that the short step between the timeless future of the Elysian fields, and the «unearthly twilight of blackest Hell» is fatally spanned by surrender to the lusts of the flesh.

Jerome van Aeken (El Bosco) painted *The Deadly Sins* as a table-top, and it is exhibited in this form, protected by a sheet of glass, in the same way as the famous *History of King David* by Hans Sebald Beham is displayed in the Louvre. It came into the possession of the Prado only quite recently from Escorial.

Within a luminous circle Christ is depicted above the words «Cave, cave, Dominus videt». Beyond this centre-piece, the panel is divided into seven parts, in each of which one of the Seven Deadly Sins is represented. On the four corners of the table there is an allegorical representation of Death, The Last Judgment, Hell, and Paradise. *The Deadly Sins* was greatly admired by Philip IInd, who ordered that it should be kept in the room in which he later died.

El Bosco used to describe these pictures as dreams, and the German critic Charles Justi remarks «a wild and violent blending of dream and reality, executed in a thoughtful and painstaking style». These occasional flights into a nightmare world of their own is to be observed in many other brilliant artists, such as Callot, David Teniers and Goya. Contemporaries often attacked *El Bosco's* work on the ground that he selected fantastic themes so as to disguise his inability to portray the things his eyes actually saw, but the indications are that many artistic geniuses are haunted by similar grotesque and macabre shapes. Psychologically speaking, these «dream pictures» show his tremendous preoccupation with all the aspects and consequences of sin, and his triptychs nearly always follow the same form; the left-hand panel being concerned with the origin of sin, the right-hand one with its consequences, and the main, central, panel with the unending struggle between Good and Evil for possession of the human soul.

El Bosco has sometimes been called «the remote ancestor of the caricaturist», and there is a certain burlesque quality in his small picture, known as *The Extraction of the Stone of Madness,* which King Philip IInd. bought from the heirs of Don Felipe de Guevara.

Another panel showing the temptations suffered by the patriarch of the Tebaida monks is interesting, but inferior to his triptych on the same theme in Lisbon.

Commenting upon *El Bosco's* unusual personality a Prior of the Escorial monastery wrote during the XVIIIth. century «beneath the guise of pictures apparently designed solely to give pleasure to the beholder he imparts a religious message of tremendous power. The effectiveness of his work lies largely in his capacity for the most exact copies from Nature, especially of birds and fishes, together with a brilliantly conceived sense of fantasy, which often makes it difficult to distinguish one from the other».

Even with only four examples of his work Albrecht Dürer manages to demonstrate his mastery as a portrait painter. There is a self-portrait; that of an unknown man, and two separate nudes representing Adam and Eve. His self-portrait, dated 1498, was

Santo Domingo de Silos.

El Cardenal.   The Cardinal.
Le Cardinal.   Der Kardinal.

La Virgen de la Rosa.   The Virgin of the Rose.
La Vierge de la Rose.   Madonna mit der Rose.

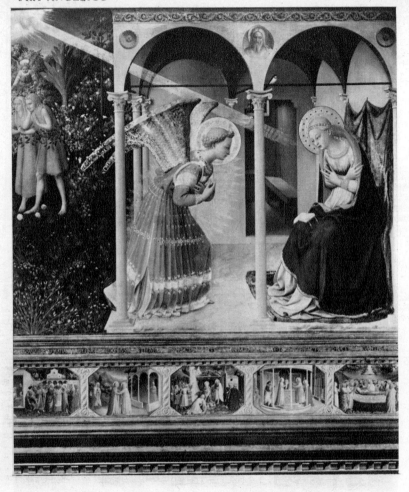

La Anunciación.   The Annunciation.
L'Annonciation.   Die Verkündigung.

Historia de Nastagio degli Honesti (fragmento).
Histoire de Nastagio... (détail).
The Story of Nastagio... (detail).
Die Geschichte von Nastagio... (fragment).

Angel músico.   Angel Musician.
Ange musicien.   Musizierender Engel.

El Tránsito de la Virgen. The Death of the Virgin Mary.
La Dormition de la Vierge. Der Tod der heiligen Jungfrau.

Noli me tangere.

La Virgen, el Niño, un Santo y un Angel.
La Vierge, l'Enfant, un Saint et un Ange.
The Virgin, and Child, with a Saint and Angel.
Madonna mit Kind, Heiligen und Engel.

PALMA «EL VIEJO»

La Adoración de los Pastores.   The Adoration of the Shepherds.
L'Adoration des Bergers.   Die Anbetung der Hirten.

PAOLO VERONESE

Jesús y el Centurión.   Jesus and the Centurion.
Jésus et le Centurion.   Jesus und der Centurion.

Venus y Adonis.   Venus and Adonis.
Vénus et Adonis.   Venus und Adonis.

Moisés salvado del Nilo.   Moses rescued from the Nile.
Moïse sauvé du Nil.   Moses vom Nil gerettet.

Mater Dolorosa.

Salomé.

TIZIANO

Venus recreándose con la música.
Vénus se récréant avec la musique.

Venus listening to music.
Venus und der Orgelspieler.

bought by King Philip IVth. from King Charles Ist, of England. Prior to that it had been the property of Nüremberg Town Hall, and also of the British Earl of Arundel, and only reached the Prado in 1827. Perhaps the most interesting characteristic revealed by this self-portrait is the blending of the stern German character with softer Italian influences of light and colour.

The less well-known *Portrait of an Unknown Man* is also in the artist's best vein, and the ruddy complexion, keen eyes, and tightly compressed lips combine to produce a brilliant character sketch. This picture, dated 1524, is recorded in the inventory of the Alcázar de Madrid in 1686, finally reaching the Prado in 1827. At that time the experts were not convinced, as they now are, that it was the work of Dürer himself, classifying it as the work of one of his pupils.

Dürer's figures of Adam and Eve, painted in 1507, first came to Spain as a gift from Queen Christina of Sweden to King Philip IVth. but narrowly escaped being burned as obscene during the reign of the prudish King Charles IIIrd. They were hidden in the Academia de San Fernando until they were brought to the Prado in 1827. Incidentally, various copies of these pictures, containing minor variations, are to be seen in the Uffizi Gallery in Florence. It is interesting to note that these are the earliest known oil paintings of Adam and Eve, with the sole exception of he left panel of Van der Weyden's triptych *The Redemption*.

The *Portrait of an Old Man*, which is exhibited among Dürer's nudes, is believed by some experts to be the work of Hans Holbein (the Younger) and, if they are correct, this Hall XLIV contains specimens of the two greatest German Masters. It is a portrait of extraordinary power, believed to represent Sebastian Munster, but mystery surrounds the identity of both painter and model. There is a copy of this painting in the Philadelphia Museum and, although some critics attribute it to Joos van Cleve, modern opinion i increasingly convinced that it is by Holbein.

In this same Hall there are two pictures by Lucas Cranach *(the Elder)* portraying a hunting scene, and two others entitled *The Three Graces* and *The Ages and Death of Man*, by Hans Baldung, but none of these will bear comparison with the surrounding

Flemish and German masterpieces. Van Hemesen's *The Surgeon* reveals the characteristic Flemish style, and, finally, there is a rather colourless head and shoulders portrait by a disciple of François Clouet which, being French, seems oddly out of place.

VESTIBULE TO THE CENTRAL GALLERY (HALL XXIV)

We enter this Vestibule by crossing the Rotunda, where four XVth. century Spanish painters profit by a fine direct light. These are Pedro Berruguete, Bartolomé Bermejo, Fernando Gallego and «Juan de Flandes», though there are also two outstanding masterpieces by unknown artists, entitled *The Virgin of the Catholic Monarchs* and *The Archangel Michael.*

Coming direct from the work of the Flemish school, the inevitable comparison is unfavourable to the Spanish masters who, although they sought to model themselves upon such painters as Van der Weyden and *El Bosco,* had not achieved an equal mastery of design and management of colour. Perhaps the more highly strung Spanish temperament is less in sympathy with the extraordinary attention to detail achieved by northern artists.

The Virgin of the Catholic Monarchs clearly reveals Flemish influence. It was almost certainly commissioned by the famous Inquisitor Torquemada for the Convent of St. Thomas in Avila in the year of the discovery of America. From Avila it passed to the Quinta del Duque del Arco, then to the Museo de la Trinidad, finally reaching the Prado in 1872.

In May 1952 the Prado Museum bought four beautiful pannels by Juan de Flandes, famous Flemish painter. They represent: *The Resurrection of Lazarus, The Prayer in the Garden of Gethsemane, The Ascension of Christ* and *The Descent of the Holy Spirit.* They are of the same size, and came to the Prado from Saint Lazarus Church of Palencia.

Juan de Flandes painted for Queen Isabel the Catholic from 1496 up to 1510, when he died in Palencia. Some historians believe that Juan de Flandes is the same John Sallaert, called «One Master» who worked in Ghent in 1480.

The artist of the *Virgin of the Catholic Monarchs*, being unknown, has been given the name of Zafra, after the village of his birth. His second picture in the Prado is, therefore, known as *The St. Michael of Zafra*, being brought to the Prado in 1925 from the Hospital of St. Michael in Zafra.

The war-like figure of the young St. Michael, surrounded by good and evil angels, is immediately arresting, and closer examination reveals a mass of brilliantly portrayed detail. The slimy quality in the skins of the demons, and the metallic shades of the Saint's armour and shield are uncannily realistic.

This picture, originally painted on a panel, was transferred to canvas only after it came into the possession of the Prado. It was painted late in the XVth. century by an Andalusian Master, and again reveals the contemporary Flemish influence.

Berruguete, father of the great sculptor Alonso, was the first Spanish painter to study in Italy, and the Prado contains a number of panels by him illustrating scenes from the lives of St. Domingo de Guzmán, and of the Italian martyr Pedro of Verona. Perhaps the most interesting of these represents the «auto de fe» held in Avila on November 16th. 1491.

XVth. century Spanish painting was still under foreign influences, Berruguete's work revealing the Italian, while that of Bermejo, and Gallego follows the Flemish Masters, but already it is possible to discern a purely Spanish tendency in search of a faithful copy direct from Nature.

Berruguete's ten panels were, like Zafra's *Virgin of the Catholic Monarchs*, commissioned by the Convent of St. Thomas in Avila. That representing the «auto de fe» was the property of Don Ignacio Jugo until 1867, when it was sold to the Spanish Government and placed first in the Museo de la Trinidad and, finally, in the Prado.

The other nine panels came into the possession of the Museo de la Trinidad when, in 1836, the Government seized the property of certain religious communities. Four of these panels originally formed the altarpiece, dedicated to St. Domingo, in the Convent of St. Thomas at Avila. These are the centrepiece, *St. Domingo de Guzmán*, *St. Domingo and the Albigenses*, *St. Domingo's Miraculous Cure of a Young Man* and *The Revelation of the Virgin Mary*. Other panels portray *The Sermon*, *The Prayer*, *The Death* and *The Burial* of the Martyr.

Some critics claim to distinguish a certain inequality in Berruguete's style in these panels, and suggest that some obviously inferior sections were the work of his pupil Santacruz, or Santos Cruz. The XIXth. century French critic, Paul Lefort, wrote «the quality of the ten panels is far from homogeneous, revealing one artist clearly more gifted than the other, and it is for their vigorous colour, rather than for their occasionally faulty design, that they bring to mind the early works of the Venetian School».

On the other hand, the German critic August Mayer considers these panels to be Berruguete's supreme masterpiece, and writes, «these pictures effectively refute the charge that Spain produced no great primitive painters».

The best of the series of panels are the «auto de fe»; *St. Domingo and the Albigenses*, and *The Martyr St. Peter at Prayer*. Those in which the inferior work of another artist in most obvious are *The Sermon of St. Peter*, *The Martyrdom of St. Peter* and *The Revelation of the Virgin Mary*.

The *St. Domingo of Silos*, by Bartolomé Bermejo, is of particular interest because of the remarkable beauty of the filigreed background, and the small symbolic figures grouped behind the dominating representation of the Saint. The same meticulous attention to detail is displayed in the painting of the embroidered and jewelled mitre, while the powerful portrayal of the Saint's expression again reveals the Flemish tradition.

This example of Bermejo's work has been described as «the most striking of any Spanish primitive painting». It came originally from a Daroca convent, being brought to Madrid in the 1870's for the National Archaeological Museum, and reached the Prado in 1922. It formed the centre-piece of the main retable in the Daroca convent, being commissioned in 1474 and terminated in 1477.

The critic Don Elías Tormo writes of *St. Domingo of Silos* «a glance at this panel is sufficient to convince us that Bermejo is not just another painter of religious subjects, but is the first of the Spanish portraitists». It is interesting to note the liberal use made by the artist of gold, which he employs in robes, furniture, woodwork and numerous other details of the background.

Fernando Gallego's *The Blessing of Christ* cannot stand comparison with the work of Bermejo, but it is restful after *St. Domingo of Silos* for its contrasting lack of detail and ornamentation. It originally formed the central panel in a retable of the Church of San Lorenzo in Toro, being painted in about the year 1490. It came to the Prado in 1915 as part of a legacy from Señor Bosch, who had bought it in Paris from a collector by the name of Kleinberger, who had discovered it years before in a church in Zamora. The influence of the Van Eycks is unmistakable.

In this same Gallery there are a number of interesting panels by unknown artists originally in the Carthusian Monastery at Miraflores, which came into the possession of the Prado at the time of the dispersal of the Museo de la Trinidad. They represent *The Visitation* and *The Nativity, The Sermon on the Mount, The Arrest and Beheading of St. John the Baptist*. Some critics have ascribed them to Gallego, and it is obvious that they belong to the Flemish-Spanish School and period.

> At this point visitors may either continue on through the Gallery, or may again cross the Rotunda to enter the left wing of the building where, in 12 Galleries, the hundred and fifty best Italian pictures in the Prado may be seen. In our opinion the second alternative ist the better, and we therefore continue with the Gallery marked II, devoted to Raphael.

HALL II

In this Hall, against a background of red velvet, a number of Raphael's picture are exhibited. These are, firstly, *The Cardinal*, painted in 1510 and bought by King Charles IVth. which reached the Prado in 1827 from the Royal Palace at Aranjuez.

It has never been possible definitely to identify the subject of this portrait.

Secondly, *The Holy Family (del Cordero)* which is a signed panel dated 1517, coming to the Prado from Escorial in 1837.

Thirdly, *The Visitation;* a panel believed to have been painted in about 1519, which was transferred to canvas in Paris in 1816. This is also a signed work of Raphael from the Escorial, having been bought by King Philip IVth. in 1655. Critics have suggested that one of Raphael's pupils, Perino del Vaga, collaborated with his master in painting this picture.

Fourthly, *Christ's Fall on the Road to Calvary.* This panel, painted and signed in about 1517, was also transferred to canvas in Paris between the years 1816 and 1818. In 1661 King Philip IVth. paid the Convent of St. Maria dello Spasimo in Palermo, an annual pension of four thousand ducats, and the picture was sent by them to Spain at his request, being transferred to the Prado from the Royal Palace in 1821. Again critics detect the intervention of one of Raphael's pupils, in this case Julius Romano or Penni.

Fifthly, *The Virgin (del Pez),* painted in 1513, which was also transferred to canvas. In 1638 it was sent by the Neapolitan Church of Santo Domingo to the Duke of Medina de las Torres, who presented it to King Philip IVth. It reached the Prado from El Escorial in 1837, and also shows signs of Giulio Romano's collaboration.

Sixthly, *The Holy Family*—often called *The Pearl*—which was painted around 1518. This once formed part of King Charles Ist's famous collection of paintings and, after the British King's execution, was bought by King Philip IVth. for £2.000. Its popular name arose from King Philip's comment, «This is the pearl of my collection», even though it also reveals signs of the work of one or more of Raphael's pupils.

Lastly, *The Holy Family (del Roble),* which was painted in 1518; a duplicate being in the Pitti Gallery in Florence. It reached the Prado from the Royal Palace in Madrid in 1827.

In the same Hall there are various other pictures of minor importance.

Raffaello Sanzio, or Santi (Raphael) died in 1520 at the age of 37, but before his death he achieved universal success and recognition, being acknowledged as the head of a School of painting which has unquestionably exerted a powerful influence upon world art. Admirers and imitators appeared in many European countries, among them the so-called Valencian School of Juan de Juanés.

Admiration for his work continued undiminished until the beginning of the XIXth. century and, although today less pronounced, he is still recognised as one of the supreme products of the Italian Renaissance. His style can be directly traced to that of his master Pietro Perugino, but he contrived to assimilate all the best qualities of the period, even including that of his greatest rival for Papal favour, Michael Angelo. In later years various of Raphael's pupils and imitators faithfully copied his technique, but none, in our opinion, ever possessed his genius or achieved his mastery of every form of artistic expression, oil-painted panels, frescos, murals, altar-pieces, and even delicate miniatures.

The Holy Family (del Cordero), which is only 29 × 21 cm., is perhaps the supreme example of his work as a miniaturist. Experts may point out that it reveals the influence of Leonardo da Vinci, or that the figure of St. Joseph follows the tradition of Fra Bartolommeo, but the fact remains that it reveals Raphael as one of the greatest artists of all time.

The Holy Family hardly justifies King Philip IVth's claims on its behalf, despite its undoubted beauty and probably, *The Virgin of the Rose* is an even better example of Raphael's style Critics of all nationalities, however, seem to be in agreement that the *Virgin (del Pez)*, together with his *Madonna of San Sixto*, at present in Dresden, are the most perfect of Raphael's altar-pieces.

The large painting *Christ's Fall on the Road to Calvary* was valued far higher than any other of his works in 1834, when it was priced at no less than 4.000.000 «reales». To present-day eyes it seems too sombre in its colouring, but the authentic touch of the Master is clearly revealed in the portrayal of Christ and the Virgin Mary.

Raphael's *Portrait of a Cardinal* is considered by many people to be his finest portrait, and all agree that it was untouched by any brush but his own. It is the pale and intelligent head of a typical Renaissance Cardinal, a brilliant study of character, revealing a subtle mastery of colour and tone.

HALL III

The most notable exhibits of this Hall are Botticelli's *The Story of Nastagio degli Honesti* and Fra Angelico's *The Annunciation*.

The Annunciation, is a panel believed to have been painted between the years 1430 and 1445, and was sold by the Convent of Santo Domingo at Fiesole to the Duke of Lerma in 1611. After a period in the Convent of Descalzas Reales in Madrid it reached the Prado in 1861. It shows five episodes in the life of the Virgin Mary, closely resembling those by the same artist in the Convent of St. Mark in Florence, and also in Cortona.

The three panels by Botticelli, painted in 1483 or 1487, belong to a series of four, of which the other is on exhibition in London, and were inspired by incidents in Bocaccio's *The Decameron*. They reached the Prado in December 1941 as a legacy from Don Francisco Cambó, who bought them from the Spiridon Gallery in Berlin in 1929.

It is interesting to note that this *Annunciation* is the only example of Fra Angelico's work in the Prado. However, it is a worthy one, revealing the inimitable, dreamlike quality which made the friar unique even in the Florence of the early XVth. century. In his treatment of religious subjects Fra Angelico achieved a spirituality—a tender delicacy of expression, gesture and form—which no other artist has ever been able to equal. In the words of the critic Denis, «Fra Angelico used colours that had been blended with the light of Paradise».

While Fra Angelico's work reveals his own deep spiritual serenity, Botticelli's unmistakably expresses the artist's profound restlessness. Sandro Botticelli was a creature of his times, when Lorenzo de Medici's love of splendour was in mortal conflict with the austerity of Savonarola, and his work clearly reflects this ideological struggle. Even when painting religious subjects there is an almost pagan appreciation of the world of the senses: Virgins and

Venuses alike being chosen solely for their physical beauty rather than for any qualities of spirituality or intelligence.

The Botticelli panels in the Prado were commissioned to decorate the bridal chamber of a daughter of a noble Florentine family, and some critics have expressed the view that, while he was responsible for their design, he left much of the actual painting to his pupils.

The Story of Nastagio degli Honesti is not a good example of Botticelli's work though, even so, it still reveals occasional touches of the Master's hand.

HALL IV

The most notable work here is *The Death of the Virgin Mary*, a small panel by Andrea Mantegna. However, there are also two extremely interesting panels by one of the earliest painters represented in the Prado, the Florentine Taddeo Gaddi who was born in 1300 and died in 1366. They depict scenes from the life of St. Eloy, and were a legacy from Don Francisco Cambó in 1941.

There is also a fresco, by Melozzo da Forli, entitled *The Angel of Music*, belonging to the early XVth. century Florentine School. A painting by Giovanni dal Ponte, in the form a frieze, represents the seven liberal arts of Astronomy, Geometry, Arithmetic, Music, Rhetoric, Logic and Grammar. Each of these allegorical figures is accompanied by a portrait of the man considered by the artist to be most eminent in that particular art or science Ptolemy, Euclid, Pythagoras, Tubalcain (the inventor of the organ), Cicero, Aristotle and Donato or Prisciano.

Mention may also be made of two interesting Venetian pictures *The Virgin and Child between two Saints*, by Giovanni Bellini, and *Christ giving the Keys to St. Peter*, by Vicenzo Catena. The former came to the Prado in 1821, having formed part of the collection of King Philip Vth.; the latter—at that time mistakenly attributed to Giorgione—being brought from El Escorial in 1839. There is a duplicate of this on exhibition in Boston.

The Prado is fortunate in possessing one of the world's few authentic Mantegna oil-paintings, *The Death of the Virgin*, believ-

ed to have been painted around 1462. It was bought by King
Philip IVth. when, under the Protectorate, the collection of King
Charles Ist. of England was put up for auction. Formerly in the
Royal Palace at Madrid, it came to the Prado in 1821.

The grouping of the Apostles around the figure of the dead
Virgin Mary, and the powerful portrayal of expression on their
faces, the whole scene set against a grey landscape, is extraordinarily moving, and no visitor should fail to see it.

HALL V

This contains seven works by Andrea del Sarto, two by Parmigianino, two by Bernardino Luini, two by Correggio, one by
Sebastiano del Piombo and one by Bronzino.

Of special interest is the picture *La Gioconda*, which some
people believe was painted by Leonardo da Vinci, though the best
critics consider that it is only an unusually fine copy of the original, which is to be seen in the Louvre. The wood upon which
it is painted is oak, which suggests a Northern origin, but one
of the most generally held opinions today is that it is a copy made
by Leonardo's Spanish pupil, Yáñez de la Almedina. It was in
the Alcazar of Madrid at the end of the XVIIth. century, and
came to the Prado in 1828.

The Florentine painter, Andrea del Sarto, belongs to the period
when the great Italian School had passed its best, but his two
panels in the Prado are unusually interesting. The first is of four
figures—the Virgin, Child, a Saint and an Angel—, the second a
portrait of his wife, Lucrecia di Baccio, the colouring of which is
reminiscent of Raphael.

This portrait reached the Prado from the Royal Palace in 1821,
while the other, and far more important example of del Sarto's
work, was bought for £230 by King Philip IVth. for El Escorial
from King Charles Ist. of England's collection.

Andrea del Sarto, who was a contemporary of Raphael, also died
before reaching middle age and, although this altar-piece is considered one of his finest works, it is lacking in the deep religious
sentiment, which infused the paintings of the early Florentine Mas-

ters of the XVth. century, though perhaps superior to many of them in technique

Parmigianinò, who died when only 37 years old, is a severe, accurate, but not particularly inspired portrait painter, and the head and shoulders of a child, by Bronzino, reveals a similar cold mastery of detail, marred by a lack of psychological interest in his subject.

The Holy Family, by Bernardino Luini, displays this artist's usual somewhat cloying style but, in a catalogue of the paintings in El Escorial made in 1574, it was listed as a probable Leonardo da Vinci. Once the property of King Philip IInd., it was included in the Prado collection in April 1839.

The best known of Correggio's pictures in the Prado is probably his *Noli me Tangere*, which aroused an enthusiasm among the Neoclacissists which today it is a little. difficult for us to understand. This particular picture was bought by the Duke of Medina de las Torres from the collection of King Charles Ist. of England for presentation to King Philip IVth. It is believed to have been painted in 1525, and reached the Prado in 1839 from El Escorial.

Greater skill is displayed in the portrayal of Jesus than in that of Mary Magdalene, but the «sublimity» of Correggio, so often emphasised by Mengs and discussed by Bernard Berenson, is difficult to detect in this gentle idealisation of reality.

Mention must be made of Fra Sebastiano del Piombo's *Christ bearing the Cross*, which reveals the influence of Michael Angelo. A duplicate of this picture is in the Hermitage Museum in Leningrad, and is believed to have been commissioned by one of the Emperor Charles Vth's Ambassadors. It was looted by Napoleon's Marshal Soult from El Escorial, and entered the possession of the Prado in 1839.

HALL VI

This Hall contains several Italian pictures from various schools, several of them being the work of 16th. century artists. The authorship of some of these has never been fully established. However, one canvas on a religious theme is the work of Giorgio da Castelfranco (the «Giorgione») and was presented by the Duchess of Medina de las Torres to King Philip IVth., reaching the Prado from El Escorial in 1839.

St. Jerónimo and the portrait of Micer Marsilio and his wife were originally in the Madrid Alcázar, and were painted and signed by Lorenzo Lotto in 1523. *The Birth of Jesus*, acquired by King Charles IVth. is the work of Federico Barocci, and there is an interesting *Holy Family* attributed to the Florentine artist Jacopo dal Conte.

The *Noli me Tangere* is by Giulio Romano and Gian Francesco Penni, and the *Portrait of a Doctor* by Lucia Anguisciola. Others are the supposed portrait of King Alfonso IInd. by Girolamo da Carpi; *The Scourging of Christ* by an anonymous pupil of Michael Angelo and, finally, a *Holy Family* by Pontormo.

HALL VII

This is the first Hall devoted to the collection of Venetian Masters, and contains examples of the work of Titian, Palma (the Elder), Moroni, Licinio, Padovanino and Dossi.

The Adoration of the Shepherds, by Palma, came from the royal collection, where it was ascribed to a younger painter of the same School, Bonifacio Veronese, and is one of the most interesting of the numerous renderings of this particular theme.

Paintings by Titian:

Virgin and Child with two Saints, obviously inspired by Giorgione's work on the same theme, though the influence of Giovanni Bellini—master of both Giorgione and Titian—is also clearly discernible. This is one of the earliest of Titian's works, and came to the Prado from El Escorial in 1839. The Saints are believed to be St. George and St. Catherine.

Ecce Homo, which is painted on slate and signed by the artist, is believed to have been commissioned personally by the Emperor Charles Vth., who took it with him on his retirement into the Monastery of Yuste, where he died in 1558.

Christ appearing as a Gardener, painted by order of Queen

Mary of Hungary, was cut from the *Noli me Tangere* in 1566 by order of King Philip IInd.

Two *Dolorosas*, one on wood and the other on marble. The latter, a companion work to the *Ecce Homo*, bearing only a part of the Master's signature, is the finer of the two, and was sent to Queen Mary of Hungary in 1554, when she was acting as Regent of Flanders. That painted on wood is believed to have been given by Titian to the Emperor Charles Vth. in 1550, and was in his possession at the time of his death in the Monastery of Yuste. The *Dolorosa* on marble is a brilliant portrayal of grief, and was said to have «aroused pious sentiments» in the heart of the Emperor.

HALL VII A

This Hall is devoted to eight pictures by Veronese.
These are:

1) *Youth choosing between Virtue and Vice;* one of the artist's early works, of which there is a duplicate in the Frick collection in New York. It is known to have been in the possession of King Charles IInd. during the last years of the XVIIth. century, and came to the Prado in 1821.

2) *The Martyrdom of St. Mena*—formerly believed to be St. Gines—was a gift from a Spanish Admiral to King Philip IVth., and reached the Prado, from El Escorial, in 1837.

3) *The Outcast Family of Cain* is catalogued as having been in the Royal Palace in the reign of King Charles IInd. There is a duplicate in Vienna.

4) *Christ discoursing in the Temple.* This is one of the finest canvases of Veronese, and loses nothing from the belief that the background may have been painted by the artist's brother, Benedetto. It came to the Prado from the Royal Palace in 1821. When Ribera was in Italy he made a copy of this picture.

5) *The Penitent Magdalene,* dated 1583, belonged to the collection of Queen Elizabeth Farnesio, becoming the property of the Prado in 1828.

6) *Jesus and the Centurion* belongs to the period of the painter's maturity, and came to the Prado in 1839 from El Esco-

rial, having formerly been part of the collection of King Charles Ist. of England. Veronese made several duplicates of this picture.

This Hall also contains *Portraits* of Livia Colonna and Lavinia Vecellio (Titian's daughter).

Paolo Caliari was given the surname Veronés by the Spaniards after his native city of Verona. He is the third of the great Venetian triumvirate, of which Titian and Tintoretto are the others.

The work of these three artists had an exceptional influence upon Spanish artistic taste and style, directly inspiring both El Greco and Velázquez. They were the undisputed favourites of the Spanish Kings of the XVIth. and XVIIth. centuries, and it was the special enthusiasm for the Venetian triumvirate shewn by the Emperor Charles Vth. and his son Philip IInd.—especially for Titian—which is the reason why the Prado today possesses such a splendid collection of works from this School.

It is interesting to note that the influence of the Church in Spain confined the work of Spanish artists to religious subjects at a time when the Venetians of the XVIth. century were able to portray the nude in mythological themes. This prudish attitude in Spain gravely limited their scope, and it is only due to the Flemish and Italian painters of the XVIth. and XVIIth. centuries —with their liking for pagan themes—that the walls of the Prado are brightened by the flesh tints of such painters as Rubens.

One feels that religious themes were little more than an excuse for the Venetian School of painters, selected only in order to enable them to display their decorative and pictorial brilliance, and the pleasure that they give to the beholder lies in their rich colouring rather than for any religious sentiment that they convey. This is particularly true of the *Martyrdom of St. Mena,* where the exuberance of the figures depicted obscures completely the tragic scene after which it is named.

The critic, Don Pedro de Madrazo, sums up Veronese's work as follows: «His genius lies in the majesty of the figures he portrays, beautifully grouped in the classical style, and in a beauty appealing to the senses rather than to the mind, through the medium of his masterly use of colour. Veronese was not the equal of Titian

in conveying the more delicate flesh-tones, but his luminous colouring, and strange deep shadows, were never equalled by any other
of the Venetian Masters.»

HALL VIII

This Hall is entirely devoted to paintings by Titian Vecellio.
These are:

1) *The Church upheld by Spain*, and 2) *Jesus and Simon of
Cyrene*, both of which came to the Prado from El Escorial.

3) *Venus listening to music*, and 4) *The Marqués del Vasto
haranguing his Troops*. These two pictures were bought from the
collection of King Charles Ist. of England.

5) *Philip IInd. after the Battle of Lepanto commending his
son to God*. This was a companion picture to Titian's *Charles Vth.
at Mühlberg*, completed in 1575 and reaching the Prado from
the Royal Palace in Madrid.

6 and 7) Two portraits entitled *Gentleman with a Watch*, and
The man in an Ermine Collar.

8 and 9) Two pictures entitled *St. Margaret* and *St. Catherine.*

The picture *The Church upheld by Spain* is upon the same
lines as the other canvas executed by Titian for the Emperor
Charles Vth., entitled *The Church persecuted by Heresy*. During
the reign of King Philip IInd. the theme was repeated by the
artist for the Doria family, which had played a distinguished part
in the victory of Lepanto. In these later versions Titian subs-
tituted the arms of the House of Doria for those of Spain on the
shield carried by the figure fighting on behalf of religion.

The 1949 Prado catalogue relates that when, in 1566, Vasari
visited Titian, he saw an uncompleted portrait of Alfonso Ist. of
Ferrara against a similar mythological background. In 1575, after
the Battle of Lepanto, the picture was sent by Titian to Philip IInd.
and showed Spain as the Goddess Minerva—a rather surprising
addition being that of a turban to the figure of Neptune.

There are two almost identical versions in the Prado of Titian's picture, *Venus listening to music*, in one of which the Goddess
of Love is embraced by Cupid while, in the other, she is shown
fondling a small dog.

Both have had an interesting history, and were in danger of

being burned as indecent because of the nude figures, while that showing Cupid was carried off to France by Napoleon's brother, Joseph. However, both were in the Academy of San Fernando again by 1818, and came to the Prado nine years later. In 1834 they were valued at 400.000 «reales» each. The canvas containing the figure of Cupid is signed by Titian while the other is not.

It is not known who commissioned Titian to paint these two versions of *Venus listening to Music*, but one critic suggests that it may have been for Francesco Assonica. Madrazo, who believes them to have been painted between 1530 and 1540, says, «These canvases can clearly be identified with the famous *Reclining Venus* in Florence, commissioned by Francesco Maria della Rovere, Duke of Urbino, the model used in both being the same. This is particularly noticable since she is of a type not usually chosen by the artist, which suggests that she was the mistress of the Duke. There is a similar picture in the Cambridge Gallery, supposed to represent the Princess of Eboli—with King Philip IInd. at her side playing a lute—but it seems unlikely that women of the Royal family would have been willing to pose in the nude».

Titian's second version of *Jesus with Simon of Cyrene* reveals a more profound feeling for religion than is usual with him. The Christ is not the usual tragic, exhausted Man, staggering beneath the burden of the Cross and scourged by His executioners, but a gentle figure, whose features express only a serene pity for His persecutors. The expression on the face of Simon, as he gazes at the stricken figure, is profoundly moving, and this canvas is considered by most people to be the best of Titian's religious works in the possession of the Prado.

HALL VIII A

This Hall contains paintings by Veronese and Tintoretto. We can also see here the paintings: *Allegory*, by Michele Parrasio, *Santa Agueda*, by Carlo Veronese, and self-portraits of Paris Bordone and Tintoretta (Tintoretto's daughter). The following are those by Veronese:

1) *Abraham's Sacrifice of Isaac*, was bought from the collection of King Charles Ist. of England, entering the Prado in 1837

IMPORTANT NOTICE

Through gallery number VIII (Sala VIII) one may proceed to the three recently opened galleries numbered «Salas» XXVA, XXVI A and XXX A. In the first of these, 13 Italian paintings are now on exhibition, among them one by Palma «the elder», several by Titian and by Dossi, Moroni and Licinio (these works having been moved from gallery VII) as well as that by Sebastiano dei Piombo (from gallery V).

The «Sala XXVI A» is completely dedicated to Zurbarán, 19 of his works being exhibited here, among them all those which were before registered in «Sala XXV» (See pg 131) and «Sala LXII» (pg. 240). Moreover, several paintings depicting «Hercules'works» have been released from the Museum's warehouse.

The gallery XXX A brings together 22 pictures by Spanish painters of the XVI th and XVII th centuries, the works having beentransferred from several rooms of the «Planta Baja» or ground floor (Tristan, Ribalta, Puga, Rizi, Herrera «the elder», Arellano, Van der Hamen, Arias, etc.).

The changes afecting the XXV gallery (see pgs. 129 and 130) should also be noted. In that gallery we can now see two pictures of historical subjects by Jusepe Leonardo (coming from the «Rotonda»), two others by Vincencio Carducho (not shown before until now) and works by Maino, Pereda, Ribalta and Rizzio about which we have written on pages 129 to 132.

It must also be noted that several French pictures (some of them never exhibited in the Museum) have recently been moved to galleries XXXVII and XXXVIII (see pg 204 and 205), and the Italian works mentioned on those pgs have been transferred to a provisional arrangement in the aisles near gallery XXXI.

....

Certain other minor changes in the disposition of the pictures have also recently been effected in the Museum but are not detailed here.

Autorretrato (fragmento)
Portrait de l'auteur (détail).

Self-portrait (detail).
Selbstbildnis (fragment).

La Bacanal.   The Bacchanal.
La Bacchanale.   Bacchanal.

Ofrenda a la diosa de los amores.   Offering to the Goddess of Love.
Offrande à la déesse des amours.   Opfer an die Göttin der Liebe.

TIZIANO

Jesús y el Cirineo.
Jésus et le Cyrénéen.

Jesus and Simon of Cyrene.
Jesus und Simon von Kyrene.

TINTORETTO

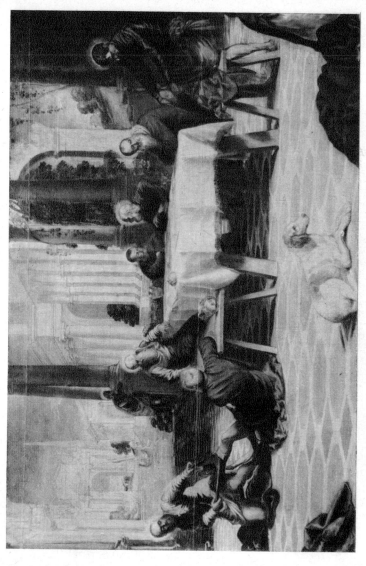

El Lavatorio (fragmento).
Le Lavement des pieds (détail).

The Washing of Feet (detail).
Die Fusswaschung (fragment).

La dama que descubre el seno.
La dame qui découvre son sein.

Lady Baring her Breast.
Die Dame enthüllt ihren Busen.

La purificación del botín de las vírgenes madianitas.
La Purification du butin des vierges madianites.
The Purification of the Booty.
Reinigen der Beute der Jungfrauen aus Madian.

TINTORETTO

Judith y Holofernes.
Judith et Holopherne.

Judith and Holofernes.
Judith und Holofernes.

JACOPO BASSANO

Entrada de los animales en el Arca de Noé.   The Animals entering Noah's Ark.
Entrée des animaux dans l'arche de Noé.   Die Tiere gehen auf die Arche Noah's

Un caballero.   Portrait of a Knight.
Un chevalier.   Ritterbildnis.

La Trinidad.   The Trinity.
La Trinité.   Die Dreifaltigkeit

La Resurrección.   The Resurrection.
La Resurrection.   Die Auferstehung.

La Adoración de los Pastores. The Adoration of the Shepherds.
L'Adoration des Bergers, Die Anbetung der Hirten.

San Andrés y San Francisco.   Saint Andrew and Saint Francis.
Saint André et Saint François.   Sankt Andreas und Sankt Franciskus.

Santa Catalina.
Sainte Catherine.

Saint Catherine.
Heilige Katharina.

JUAN DE JUANES

La última Cena
La dernière Cène

The Last Supper.
Das letzte Abendmahl

from El Escorial. There is a duplicate of this picture in Vienna,
which is considered the better of the two.

2) *Venus and Adonis*, believed to have been painted in 1580.
This canvas was bought by Velázquez when he was in Venice in
1648 on behalf of King Philip IVth. It came to the Prado in 1821
from the Royal Palace.

3) *The Wedding in Cana.* This is one of the artist's earlier
works.

4) *Susanna and the Elders*, which came to the Prado from the
Royal Palace in 1821.

5) *Discovery of the Infant Moses on the Banks of the Nile*, also
from the Royal Palace, a painting which, with its rich colouring
and masterly grouping, is one of the best of the small canvases
in the Prado. There is a beautiful painting by Veronese in the
Dresden Museum on the same subject, but the one here is equally
attractive.

HALL IX

This is devoted entirely to Titian Vecellio. Red velvet han-
gings cover the dark marble wall, and provide a magnificent
background for sixteen of Titian's finest canvases. These are:
A Self-portrait; two *Portraits of Charles Vth.;* a *Portrait of the
Empress Isabel of Portugal; a Portrait of Philip IInd; a Portrait
of Federico Gonzaga, first Duke of Mantua; The Bacchanal;
Offering to the Goddess of Love;* a large canvas entitled *Glory;*
the duplicate of *Venus listening to Music; Danäe; Salome;
St. Margaret,* and the groups *Adam and Eve, Venus and Adonis,*
and the *Burial of Christ.*

The Prado is without rival in its collection of the works of
three painters—Velázquez, Goya and Titian. Reference has already been made to no less than fourteen of Titian's canvases, and
here, in Hall IX, we have arrived at the «sancta sanctorum» of his
genius.

On the left, as we enter, there is the exquisitely coloured
Portrait of the Empress Isabel, painted in Augsburg in 1548
—nine years after the death of the Empress—the artist being
compelled to use a mediocre portrait by another artist as his

model. This portrait was originally the property of Queen Mary of Hungary, sister-in-law of the Empress Isabel, and entered the Prado in 1821.

Next to it is the technically exquisite *Portrait of Federico Gonzaga,* in which not only the head and hands, but also the texture of the coat material and every detail of the small dog, are faultlessly portrayed. It is a signed work, believed to have been painted between 1525 and 1531. Originally the property of the Marqués de Leganés, it passed to the Royal collection where, in 1666, it was priced at 200 ducats, and thence to the Prado in 1821. It was erroneously catalogued by Madrazo some years later as a portrait of Titian's patron, Alfonso d'Este, Duke of Ferrara.

Next come two splendid portraits of the Emperor Charles Vth., the larger, equestrian one, dominating the whole Hall. Beside it is a delicately executed portrait of King Philip IInd. in his early youth and, finally, a magnificent self-portrait of the Master—old and bearded—brilliantly portrayed with a striking economy of detail.

The last self-portrait to which we referred in detail was that of Dürer, and it is interesting to note the great developments in this particular branch of painting which have taken place in the 68 years between 1498 and 1566. While the German painter records his likeness by the precision of his drawing, the Venetian contrives to present us with his living image by means of a few swift strokes of his brush. Titian is known to have done three self-portraits, of which this undoubtedly the finest. It is believed to have been the property of Rubens, who bought it for the sum of 400 florins.

The Bacchanal typifies all that is best of the Venetian School and, with the *Offering to the Goddess of Love,* is unrivalled in its masterly grouping and for the tender grace of the Cupids. The sleeping Ariadne, and the whole brilliant handling of colour and design, seem to epitomise the artist's own vibrant joy of living.

The Bacchanal and the *Offering*—the latter being the smaller picture—were both signed by Titian in 1518 and, together with his *Bacchus and Ariadne* (now in the National Gallery in London), were designed to decorate the famous Alabaster Chamber of the Duke of Ferrara, husband of Lucrecia Borgia. The Duke had commissioned a *Bacchanal* by Giovanni Bellini, but the work was incomplete when that artist died and, according to Vasari, it was finished by Titian. This picture—the work of two supreme artists—was for a long time on exhibition in the Villa Aldobrandini, later becoming the property of the painter Camuccini, and finally reaching London.

The *Bacchanal* and the *Offering* in the Prado became the property of the Ludovisi family, and were for many years in the Panfili Palace at Rome. It is believed that Nicolas Ludovisi, Viceroy of Aragon, presented both works to King Philip IVth, and they reached Madrid in August, 1658.

Rubens made a copy of both pictures while he was in Italy, and these also came to Spain, after a sale in which 1.800 florins was paid for each of them. Looted during the French invasion, they passed into the possession of the Stockholm Museum in 1865.

The Offering to the Goddess of Love was originally entitled, *La Ofrenda a la Fecundidad*, and was valued at 600.000 «reales» in 1834, while its companion picture, *The Bacchanal*, was priced at 400.000 «reales». 13 years later it reached the Prado.

Writing of *The Bacchanal*, Madrazo gives the following description: «In the right foreground the beautiful figure of Ariadne is lying asleep beside a rivulet of wine, her fair hair loose around her naked body, holding an empty goblet in one hand. She is lying on her linen tunic, the end of which is draped across her arm. Beside her a youth and two Bacchantes have laid aside their lutes, while two other youths, standing beneath some trees, are taking up their song. Another more distant group of four men and a woman are dancing around a large wine jar, while they garland themselves with vine leaves. On the left a stout male figure raises a large goblet of wine to his lips, while his bearded companion, resembling an athlete from a Greek bas-relief, bears upon his shoulder a classical amphora. In the background, Theseus's ship can be seen standing out from the shore upon which he has forsaken Ariadne. The artist placed his signature on one of the recumbent Bacchantes, the model for which is believed to have been Titian's mistress, Violante. The sheet of music from which the Bacchantes have been singing has written upon it: «Qui boyt et ne reboyt il ne sait que boyre soit.» (He who drinks but once knows not the joy of drinking.)

The same critic describes *The Offering to the Goddess of Love.*

He says: «This is an allegorical representation of the joys and sorrows resulting from love. To this mystic garden two supplicant maidens have come to offer the Goddess a mirror and a votive tablet. From the base of the statue flows a stream, symbolic of fecundity, while the fruit in the tiny baskets carried by the Cupids are ornamented with precious stones.»

Don. Pedro Beroqui summed up by saying: «The *Offering* possesses a profound sense of poetry, and is perhaps one of the greatest aesthetic gifts bequeathed to us by Titian, who in it followed Leonardo's maxim: «La eccelente pittura dover sempre accrescere il diletto in chi piú la osserva.» (A great picture must always be a source of delight to those who behold it.)

The critic Frizzoni wrote, a few years ago, that the equestrian portrait of the Emperor Charles Vth. «may be considered the finest portrait in existence». To us this assertion appears dangerously categoric, though there can be no doubt as to its exceptional quality.

It was painted in Augsburg during the summer of 1548, in commemmoration of the great Protestant defeat on the river Elbe on August 24th, 1547. Writing of the Emperor Charles on this occasion an historian says: «The Emperor was riding an Andalusian horse, covered with red silk cloth. His armour was shining, and he wore the insignia of a general of the House of Burgundy—a red band, striped with gold—and in his right hand he grasped a lance. He had been suffering acutely from gout and, on the day of the battle, was extremely weak—his enemies mockingly naming him *Carlos the Moribund*, and there were many witnesses of his deathly appearance when he ordered the attack». It is an interesting historical fact that the Emperor Charles always trembled uncontrollably when his armour was being put on him but, once in battle, the delicate body became animated with the strength of courage, and his mind completely serene.

The picture was brought to Spain, together with many others, by the Emperor's sister, Mary of Hungary, and was damaged during the great fire which destroyed the Royal Palace in 1734. Even earlier than this the great canvas was harmed when, immediately, after finishing it, Titian left it in the open-air to dry,

and a gust of wind overturned it damaging the horse so seriously
that the artist himself had to carry out considerable restoration.

It came to the Prado in 1821, and in 1834 was priced for a
mere two hundred thousand «reales».

The other portrait of the Emperor Charles Vth. in the Prado
is believed to have been painted in Bologna in 1533. King Philip IVth. presented it to Charles Ist. of England, and it was
bought back for £150 at the auction which followed the execution of Charles.

Titian's portrait of King Philip IInd, painted in 1551, was
sent by the Spanish King to his aunt, Mary Tudor, at the time
of their betrothal. History records that Philip was not satisfied
with this portrait, though is it difficult to understand his criticism as it presents him as a most attractive and distinguished
young man.

Titian finished *Danaë beneath the Golden Shower* in 1552,
when he offered it to King Philip IInd. The artist had already
painted a similar picture for Duke Ottavio Farnesio, which was
the object of both praise and adverse criticism from Michael
Angelo

Not long afterwards Titian informed King Philip IInd. that
he had finished another mythological picture saying. «This will
provide a contrast with the Danaë, and help to balance its effect
in the room for which they are both intended».

This second canvas is a back view of the same nude figure
that is portrayed in the *Danaë*, and is entitled *Venus and Adonis*.
It was damaged on its way to Spain in a way that is still visible
in the centre of the picture. These two pictures, together with
the two *Reclining Venuses*, were hidden in the Academia de San
Fernando to escape their destruction by fire ordered by King
Charles IIIrd. on the grounds that they were indecent.

Titian often used his voluptuously beautiful daughter Lavinia
as his model, and we may see her as *Salome* bearing the head
of John the Baptist upon a silver dish. It is believed that *Salome*
was the property of the Marqués de Leganés, passing to the Royal
Family in 1665, and reaching the Prado in 1828.

Although we may perhaps feel that *Salome* rather notably fails to portray the horror of the occasion it represents, it yet remains an attractive example of Titian's work.

Titian's *Glory* was painted in 1551, at the orders of the Emperor Charles Vth, and reached Spain three years later. The Master entitled it *La opera della Trinitá,* and the Emperor *The Last Judgment.* It remained for many years in the Monastery of Yuste, where the Emperor Charles died in retirement, before being moved to El Escorial and receiving its present title of *Titian's Glory.*

The composition of the picture seems over-ambitious for any single canvas. It portrays the Trinity, surrounded by Angels and Seraphs, while below are numerous personalities from both the New and Old Testaments, such as Noah, Moses, David, Job, the Evangelists, and Mary Magdalene. On the right hand side of the picture can be seen the shrouded figures of Charles Vth. and his Empress, Philip IInd, Queen Mary of Hungary, and the Infanta Juana. The figure of each sinner on trial is accompanied by his guardian angel, who pleads in his defence.

Despite the sombre subject chosen by the Emperor it gives yet another opportunity to the artist to display his brilliant and colourful style.

There are two versions of *The Burial of Christ,* both signed by Titian, the better of the two being that on exhibition here, which was ordered by King Philip IInd. in 1559. A third one, which in our opinion is even more moving, is to be seen in the Louvre.

Titian's *St. Margaret,* and his group *Adam and Eve*—the latter signed by him—belong to the last period of the Master's life, when his style conformed to less exact principles.

HALL IX A

This Hall is devoted to Jacopo Robusti, universally known under his brush name of Tintoretto, adopted by him in acknowledgment of his father's profession as a dyer. He is regarded as the most dynamic of the Venetian School of painters and, despite his early poverty, lived to enjoy success and wealth.

Early in his career, Tintoretto outlined his ambition as, «the unification of Michael Angelo's drawing with Titian's use of colour». Whether or not he achieved this tremendous objective must remain a matter of opinion, but it is fairly generally agreed that Tintoretto, in the best of his work, proved himself to be one of the very greatest of the many painters produced by Italy.

Every one of Tintoretto's canvases in the Prado bears witness to his creative genius, though perhaps he never quite achieved the matchless golden hues of Titian, nor the almost mathematical exactness of design peculiar to Michael Angelo, but Tintoretto still possessed an amazing spontaneity—a kind of artistic passion—which gives to all his work an unique inspirational vitality.

This extraordinary verve seemed to carry Tintoretto over all technical obstacles, and is particularly evident on the large surfaces possible in wall painting, where his style is seen at its best.

It has been remarked that nearly all great painters fall into one of two groups, those who seek the warm golds and reds of Titian, Rubens and Rembrandt, or those who sought their ideal medium in the cold grey and sepia tones of Velázquez, Greco and Tintoretto.

The Prado contains 12 portraits and 14 other canvases by Tintoretto. Nine of these were bought by Velázquez in Venice in 1649; two—Disciples Bathing their Feet, and Paradise—immediately arresting the attention of any visitor to this Hall, both for their great size and their powerful drawing.

In our opinion, the better is Disciples Bathing their Feet —originally painted for the Venetian Church of St. Marcuola— which is an unusually vigorous picture with great attention devoted to the background. In the XVIIth. century, Father Santos wrote of this work: «The extraordinary vigour of the colours and, above all, the artist's brilliant arrangement of perspective, makes it easy to forget that we are looking at a picture, and creates the sensation that we can enter into the world that it portrays, ourselves walking through the paved court in company with the figures that the artist has portrayed.»

This work was bought at the auction of King Charles Ist's

collection, for £250. Velázquez personally arranged for its installation at El Escorial, and it was brought to the Prado only a few years ago.

Paradise—sometimes given the title *Glory*—is not one of the many preparatory sketches made by Tintoretto before he painted his large *Il Paradiso* for the Ducal Palace in Venice. It belongs to the last epoch of the Master, and was bought in Venice by Velázquez. It is in the form of a frieze, nearly 18 feet long by some 4'6" in height, crowded with so many figures that it is not easy to separate one group from another. It is dominated by the grey tones typical of Tintoretto, but suffers from being placed near the ceiling, above other pictures by him, which makes it difficult to study in detail.

It was also due to Velázquez that seven works by Tintoretto, designed to decorate the ceiling of a Venetian palace, are today in the Prado. The themes selected by the artist were from the Old Testament, and the date at which they were painted is not known. The titles given to these pictures are as follows: *The Purification of the Booty, Susanna and the Elders, Esther in the presence of Asuero, Judith and Holofernes, Queen Sheba's visit to Salomon, Joseph and Potiphar's Wife* and *The Discovery of the Infant Moses.* According to the catalogue, this series belongs to the first period of the artist's life, with the exception of the oval canvas —*The Purification*—which formed the centre piece, and which is believed to have been painted around 1570 when Tintoretto was already over 50. After their arrival in Spain these seven canvases decorated the ceiling of a bedroom in the old Alcázar de Madrid. They were saved from the destruction by fire of the old Royal Palace in 1734, when they were removed to La Granja, coming to the Prado in 1821.

The oil painting *The Purification,* is typical of Tintoretto's sweeping grey tones, and the other six canvases reveal his almost careless-seeming brilliance of technique.

Another of Tintoretto's pictures brought to Spain by Velázquez is the *Battle between Turks and Christians* which, in our opinion, is not one of the better examples of the Master's work. His

Baptism of Christ, although rather dark, is a rhythmical composition in which certain similarities to Greco have been detected. It was originally painted for the Venetian Church of San Silvestre.

The Wrath of Tarquin and *Judith and Holofernes,* though by no means Tintoretto's best work, are of great interest to the student of art, as they clearly reveal those special characteristics which brought the master fame, his handling of such a daring theme as the violation of Lucretia being typically vigorous.

Unfortunately, the quality of the work is not uniform, and our own preference is for *Judith and Holofernes,* which we believe to be one to the finest from the brush of Tintoretto, the extraordinary brilliance with which he has captured the flesh tones being almost unequalled. It was bought by King Charles IIIrd. from the collection of the Marqués de la Ensenada.

The *Woman Baring her Breast* is almost modern in its treatment and colouring, even while the head maintains the characteristics of a portrait. It is not known for certain who was the model, some critics believing that it was the painter's daughter Marietta, though others believe it to have been a famous courtesan, Veronica Franco.

Tintoretto's *Knight of the Golden Chain,* is believed to be a portrait of Paolo Veronese. In our opinion it is not so fine a work as Tintoretto's portrait of Sebastiano Veniero.

On exhibition in this Hall is a centre piece for the decoration of a ceiling painted by Tintoretto's son Domenico and entitled *Virtue Triumphing over Sin.* The Sins depicted are Lust, Spite, Treachery and Theft, which are shown in flight from the presence of Virtue, which is represented as a helmeted figure, bearing a sheaf of corn as an emblem of Peace.

HALL X A

This Hall is devoted almost entirely to the work of Bassanos, though it includes portraits by Tintoretto and Palma (the Younger).

The Bassanos were an artistic dynasty belonging to the Venetian School. There is nothing in the Prado by Francesco da Ponte, founder of the dynasty, though there are examples of the work of his more brilliant son Jacopo (1510?-1592) and of his grandsons Francesco and Leandro.

The signed *Last Supper*, by Francesco Bassano, was once in the possession of Elizabeth Farnesio. Notable among the works of Leandro are *The Miser and Lazarus* and *The Return of the Prodigal Son*, both of them being gifts to King Philip IVth. from the Duke of Medina de las Torres, though his three best canvases, in our opinion, are *Christ Expelling the Money-changer from the Temple*—numbered 27—, *Spring*, and the so far uncatalogued *Noah after the Deluge*. In the next hall there are, additionally, Jacopo Bassano's *The Punishment of Adam*, a gift from Prince Philibert of Savoy to King Philip IVth., and *The Animals entering Noah's Ark*, bought by Titian for the Emperor Charles Vth. Jacopo Bassano is today considered as one of the founders of modern landscape painting, and was unquestionably the best painter of animals produced by the Renaissance. *The Punishment of Adam* and *The Animals entering Noah's Ark* both reveal a rich vitality, though all Bassano's works strike the modern critic as being too dark. It is unfortunate that the Prado does not contain any examples of Greco's work while he was in Italy as, if it did, we believe that it would be possible to prove that the same influences were present there as are to be perceived in Jacopo Bassano's style.

It is believed that Greco was a pupil of Jacopo for a time, and some of Bassano's works reveal the same vigour and spirituality which were so marked a characteristic of the Cretan's early style.

Bassano was an indifferent draughtsman, preferring to achieve his effects by contrasting light and shade, but he is a typical master of the Venetian School of painting.

Among the portraits by Tintoretto is one believed to be of Sebastiano Veniero, who was the leader of the Venetian fleet at the great Battle of Lepanto which, in our opinion, is the finest of all the 12 portraits by Jacopo Robusti possessed by the Prado. It was presented to King Philip IVth. by the Marquess of Leganés.

Having now seen works by Titian, Veronese and Tintoretto, we must appreciate the debt we owe to the good taste in matters of Art displayed by four of the Hapsburg Kings

of Spain. It is solely due to the Emperor Charles Vth. and
to Kings Philip IInd., IIIrd. and IVth. that the Prado today
possesses one of the finest collections of the Venetian School
to be found anywhere in the world. Only by a study of them
can we fully understand the background that inspired the work
of El Greco and Velázquez.

HALLS X, XI AND XXX

This Halls is devoted to El Greco, but is really too small for
the 34 examples of his work that it contains, consisting of 24 on
religious themes and 10 portraits.

Greco's prestige has waxed and waned in a remarkable way.
Highly valued during his own life, his style ran contrary to cur-
rent opinion in the succeeding centuries and only in recent times
has it reached the pinnacle upon which it stands today. Even now
he is still a painter who provokes violent differences of opinion,
some people being rapturous about everything painted by him,
while others find his style actively repellent.

Unquestionably, after looking at a number of canvases by
other artists, with their more or less conventional methods of
presenting the human figure, it does come as something, of a
shock to be placed suddenly before one of Greco's portraits, with
its small, oval head above an immensely elongated body, and
this feeling is further emphasised by his unusual employment of
colour. There are many who claim to see nothing but deformed
shapes and caricatured likenesses but, in the case of all but a
very few, reflection reveals the profound vision of the artist, which
triumphs over—and is, in fact, emphasised by—the unique methods employed by El Greco.

The essential factor to remember is that El Greco never even
sought to paint reality, but only to transfer to canvas the state
of mind, or character, of his subject. In short, though he lived
centuries before the word was invented, Greco was the first of the
Impressionists.

Domenikos Theotokopoulos was a Cretan who learned the
art of painting in Venice at a time when Titian, though a very

old man, was still living, and when Jacopo Robusti (Tintoretto) was in his prime, and the latter's disregard for the accepted conventions of painting unquestionably had a strong influence upon El Greco. However, the popular belief that Greco originally adopted his individualistic style because he was in revolt against the conventional methods of Titian is not justified.

In fact, what happened was that after Greco had learned all that the Venetian School, as represented by Tintoretto, had to teach him, he came to Spain, where he developed its latest trends along strongly personal lines—so personal as at times almost to suggest insanity. The result was an intensely Spanish product, mystical and passionate, which seems to infuse his figures with a strange inner vibration, as though some occult power was withdrawing the soul from the already exhausted bodies.

To understand Greco, it is necessary to leave the world of design and form, and enter that of spiritual ideas. If we can achieve this the dynamic force behind the vivid, yet trembling, line of his figures reveals the unquiet mind or spirit of the subject as no other painter has ever succeeded in doing. Once this is experienced it is difficult to return to the conventional pink and white portraits of the living flesh which, by contrast, seem hopelessly insipid.

Neither of Greco's two greatest pictures are in the Prado, these being *The Burial of the Count of Orgaz*, and *The Martyrdom of St. Maurice*, but there are a sufficient number here to enable us to form a comprehensive idea of his work. Though his very earliest paintings are still mostly in Italy, the Prado contains examples from each one of the different phases though which his painting passed during his life in Spain.

One of Greco's biographers divides the Artist's work into the folloving periods: first, from the year 1577 until 1584, which was immediately after his arrival in Spain; the second—and probably the greatest—from 1584 to 1604, and the last until his death in 1614.

Of the pictures by El Greco in the possession of the Prado the following belong to the first period:

The Trinity, The Annunciation, Portrait of a Physician and

The Knight with his Hand on his Breast. Of these *The Trinity* is
known to have been painted for the Church of Saint Domingo in
Toledo not later than 1579, when his work for the altar retable
there ended, and is probably the earliest of all Greco's works in
the Prado.

Five more belong to the second period of 1584-1594, being
two *Portraits of an Unknown Man* (Nos. 806 and 813), *St. Benito, The Crucifixion* and *The Resurrection.* There are some critics
who believe that these last two canvases belong to a later period.

It seems fairly certain that the following 12 works were com-
pleted between 1594 and 1604: *Portrait of Don Rodrigo Vázquez,
St. Paul, St. Anthony of Padua, St. John the Evangelist, Christ
Bearing the Cross;* the head and shoulders *Virgin Mary, The
Divine Countenance, The Baptism of Christ, The Holy Family,
The Coronation of the Virgin Mary* and also *A Santiaguista with
St. Louis King of France,* and *St. John the Evangelist and St. Fran-
cis of Assisi.*

Finally, painted in the last 10 years of Greco's life, there
are two *Portraits of an Unknown Gentleman* (Nos. 810 and 811),
Jerónimo de Cevallos, Portrait of a Monk—believed to be of the
painter Maino—*St. Francis of Assisi with Friar Leone, Pentecost,*
and *The Adoration of the Shepherds.*

The Prado also contains the following canvases by El Greco
which it has been impossible to assign to any particular period
in the artist's life: *St. Andrew and St. Francis,* and the three
head and shoulder paintings entitled *Jesus, St. James the Elder*
and *St. Philip and St. Paul.* In order to appreciate the essential
quality of Greco's religious paintings it is only necessary to study
The Trinity, The Annunciation, Christ Bearing the Cross; the
figures of *St. Francis and St. Andrew, The Resurrection, The Crucifixion, The Baptism of Christ, Pentecost* and *The Adoration.* In
all these the artist's unique manner of emphasising the spiritual,
rather than the physical, characteristics of his subjects are to be
seen. The elongated figures, whose bodily existence seems to be in
process of visible withdrawal from the world of the flesh into that
of the spirit, are the portrayal of something which no other artist
has ever even attempted, let alone achieved.

Then there are Greco's portraits, of which he painted very
few, mostly of men. There are eight in the Prado, all of them

painted while the artist lived in Toledo, which reveal the slender and austere countenances of the Castilian aristocracy at the time when Spain was at the peak of her power.

In our opinion, the finest is the *Head of an Unknown Gentleman*, numbered 806, which is a far more masterly presentation of character than the more famous *Knight with his Hand on his Breast*, where the artist's genius was devoted to the portrayal of the hand rather than to the face of his model. Next to the *Portrait of an Unknown Gentleman*, perhaps the three best are those of *Jerónimo de Cevallos, The Unknown Physician* and the small canvas of a monk, all of which, while clearly marked by Greco's characteristic style, are intensely «alive». The half-length *Unknown Physician* is particularly effective in its sober austerity of black, white and ochre. Probably the poorest of Greco's portraits in the Prado is that of Don Rodrigo Vázquez, where both colour and design appear unconvincing.

All 8 of Greco's portraits came here from one or other of the Royal collections—two from the Alcázar de Madrid, and the other six from the country house of the Dukes of Arcos, formerly the property of the King. Five of the eight are signed and one of them is known to have been in the studio of Velázguez at the time of that artist's death in 1660.

The following of Greco's canvases reached the Prado from the Museo de la Trinidad in 1872: *St. Benito, St. Francis and St. John the Evangelist, St. Anthony of Padua, St. Francis of Assisi with Friar Leone, Christ Bearing the Cross, The Baptism of Christ, The Resurrection, Pentecost* and *The Crucifixion*. All but the first two of these are signed by the artist.

The Trinity was bought for 15.000 «reales» by King Ferdinand VIIth. from the sculptor Valeriano Salvatierra in 1827, and is not catalogued in the Prado until 1843.

The Annunciation was bought in 1868 by Doña Concepción Parody for 150 «escudos», ant *St. John the Evangelist* was presented to the Prado in 1921 by Doctor Cabañas. *St. Paul* was in the Royal collection and, after the destruction by fire of the Alcázar in 1734, hung in the Retiro Palace, first appearing in the Prado catalogue for the year 1858. *The Santiaguista with St. Louis, King of France*, which has suffered at the hands of restorers, was bequeathed to the Prado by Don Luis de Erŗazu in 1926, and *The Coronation of the Virgin Mary*, together with the possible portrait of Maino, were also recent legacies.

The *St. Andrew and St. Francis*, although signed by the artist, was completely unknown until 1937. It was presented to the Madrid Monastery of the Encarnación in 1676 by a daughter of the Duke of Abrantes when she became a nun, and it entered the Prado in 1942. *The Holy Countenance* came to the Prado in 1944 from the Mostoles Church, where its presence had been noted by Cossío.

The Saviour, St. James the Elder and *St. Philip and St. Paul* —all unknown until recent times—were acquired as late as 1946.

In 1956 the Museum acquired the wonderful painting *The Adoration of the Shepherds* which had belonged, since it was painted to the Convent of Santo Domingo el Antiguo, in Toledo.

The canvas *St. Andrew and St. Francis*, showing the standing figures of the two Saints, is the equal of any of Greco's religious paintings. Here there is his special use of brilliant, yet cold, colours, and the strange elongation of the bodies, giving them the intense, yet deathlike, air with which the artist envisaged the heroes of Christian legend. With the possible exception of Fra Angelico there is no other artist in all the Prado collection who reveals Greco's capacity for depicting the purely spiritual feelings of his subjects. Greco rarely used a human model, drawing his saints from his own imagination, half-dream, half-fantasy. On the other hand, a Saint painted by Ribera, Murillo, Zurbarán or Ribalta —not to mention countless non-Spanish artists—is nearly always a faithful representation of the man who served as his model. Not for nothing was Greco known as the «painter of souls». During the XVIIIth. and XIX th. centuries Greco's prestige sunk very low indeed, and there is hardly a critic of the period who does not refer disparagingly to the peculiarities of his style. Ponz, Ceán Bermúdez and the Madrazo brothers, all spoke of him with distaste, and Cruzada Villaamil wrote in the 1865 catalogue of the Museo de la Trinidad: «It is obvious that El Greco was insane, and his works clearly reveal the extent of his madness even though, behind his weird exaggerations, there are indications, in his handling of colour and portrayal of expression, of genius such as has been possessed by only the greatest Masters.»

In the Prado's 1872 catalogue Don Pedro de Madrazo wrote

of Greco: «He suddenly changed the style that he had acquired
from studying Titian, and began to paint as though he were a
madman. Some people believe that the change was provoked by
a desire to demonstrate his complete originality but, whatever the
motives, he totally changed his style and developed a fantastic
manner of drawing which, together with the use of livid colouring, presented his subjects as though they were half-spectres,
half-nightmares, in a way which is particularly noticeable in his
St. Maurice.»

There have been many attempts to find a purely material
explanation for Greco's strange attenuated figures, one of them
being that he suffered from some defect in his eye-sight, which
caused him to see his fellow-creatures in the distorted form which
he portrays.

Such explanation, though attractively simple, are never convincing, and what the neo-classicists called Greco's «madness» is
today revered as his «profound psychological perception».

The modern view is that, in order to depict the super-human,
spiritual qualities of saint and martyr, Greco evolved a mystical
technique of his own which, since it dealt with other-worldly subjects, could not be limited by the accepted rules and regulations
that suffice for those who seek only to portray the material world
of the flesh.

Although the seed of Greco's style may be detected in the Venetian School, he evolved into something unique. Not only is
this true of his design and drawing, but also of his use of colour.
At a time when all the world was striving to imitate the warm
golden hues of the Venetian School, Greco first—and later Velázquez—selected cold blues, greys and sepias to achieve his effects.
To appreciate this to the full it is perhaps necessary to see *St. Maurice* and *The Dream of Philip IInd.* which are still in the Monastery of El Escorial—though there is reason to hope that they
will soon be added to the Prado collection.

Don Jerónimo Seisdedos, one of the group of skilled restorers
employed in the Prado, is of the opinion that Greco treated his
canvases with distemper, following the system of the Venetian
School, and only used oil for the final touches. Probably for this
reason all of Greco's works are today in the same condition as
they were nearly three and a half centuries ago.

La Infanta Isabel Clara Eugenia.   The Infanta Isabel Clara Eugenia.
L'Infante Isabelle Claire Eugénie.   Die Infantin Isabel Clara Eugenia.

Cristo abrazando a S. Bernardo.   Christ Embracing St. Bernard.
Le Christ étreignant Saint Bernard.   Christus umarmt Sankt Bernhard.

La Epifanía.　　　　The Epiphany.
L'Epiphanie.　　　　Dreikönigstag.

Recuperación de Bahía del Brasil (fragmento).
La Récupération de Bahía, au Brésil (détail).
The Recovery of Bahia, in Brazil (detail).
Wiedereroberung von Bahia in Brasilien (fragment).

La Trinidad.   The Trinity.
La Trinité.   Die Dreifaltigkeit.

El martirio de San Bartolomé. The Martyrdom of Saint Bartholomew.
Le martyre de Saint Barthélémy   Marter des Sankt Bartholomäus.

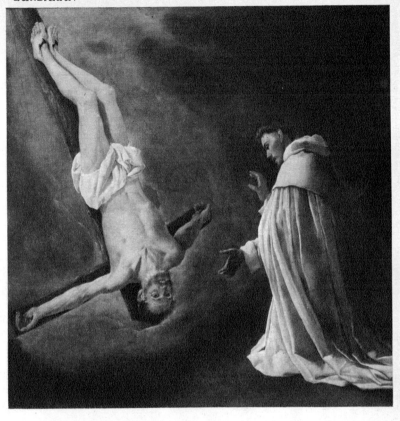

Aparición de S. Pedro a S. Pedro Nolasco.
Vision de Saint Pierre Nolasque.

Vision of St. Peter Nolasco.
Visionen des Heiligen Petrus Nolasco

Santa Casilda.   St. Casilda.
Sainte Casilde.   Heilige Casilda.

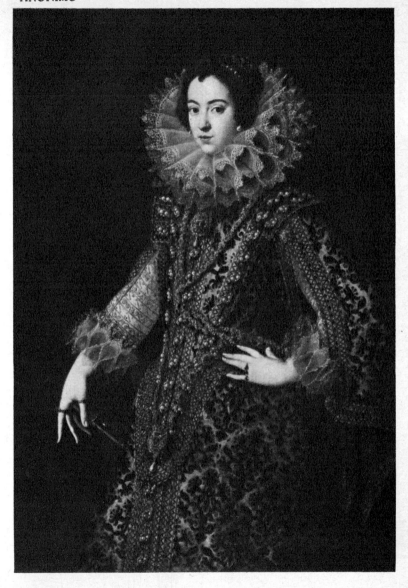

La Reina Isabel de Borbón.   The Queen Elizabeth of Bourbon.
La Reine Isabelle de Bourbon.   Königin Isabella von Bourbon.

San Pedro libertado por un ángel.   St. Peter Freed by an Angel.
Saint Pierre libéré par un ange.   Sankt Petrus von einen Engel befreit.

Cristo crucificado.   Christ on the Cross.
Le Christ crucifié.   Christus am Kreuz.

VELAZQUEZ

Los borrachos.
Les ivrognes.

The Topers.
Die Trinker.

VELAZQUIEZ

La rendición de Breda.
La reddition de Breda.

The Surrender of Breda.
Die Übergabe von Breda.

Retrato de Felipe IV.   Portrait of Philip IV.
Portrait de Philippe IV.   Bildnis von Philipp des IV.

Retrato de Martínez Montañés (fragmento).
Portrait de M. Montañés (détail).
Portrait of M. Montañés (detail).
Bildnis von M. Montañés (fragment).

El bufón D. Juan de Austria.   The Jester D. Juan de Austria.
Le bouffon D. Juan de Austria.   Der Hofnarr D. Juan de Austria.

After the visit to Greco's Halls it is, in our view, better not to go straight on to a study of Velázquez. We have, therefore, preferred to take a glance at Sections XXV and XXVI in the Prado's great Central Gallery, where are to be found the Spanish artists, namely Ribalta, Maino, Ribera, Zurbarán, Friar Juan Rizi, Pereda and Jusepe Leonardo.

CENTRAL GALLERY

SECTIONS XXV AND XXVI

Francisco Ribalta, born in Spain's «Levante», and generally regarded as a disciple of Juan de Juanes, has only recently been given the attention that his work undoubtedly deserves.

Early in his career Ribalta decided to break away from the fashion prevailing among his Spanish contemporaries, who were still wholly under the influence of Raphael, and to return to a more realistic style. It is true to say, therefore, that, although to a less notable extent than El Greco, Ribalta was equally representative of the transitional period, and so shares with the great Cretan the credit for having laid the foundations for the masterpieces of the 16th, century—the Golden Age of Spanish Art.

In a recent book, Don Carlos Espresati says that Ribalta «felt from the beginning the vital need to present the human figure in true perspective, without the conventional tricks of vague outline and half-tones popularized by the contemporary Roman School, and to portray his models with brilliant realism, so that they stand out unequivocally from their surroundings».

Ribalta has been accused of «tenebrism»—that love of obscure backgrounds of which Caravaggio was the supreme exponent in Italy—and of this Espresati remarks, «Tenebrism developed simultaneously in both Spain and Italy in a way that can only be accounted for by the basic temperamental similarity that existed between the two artists».

Ribalta's *St. Francis of Assisi Comforted by Angelic Music* is strikingly realistic in its treatment though, in our opinion, his *Christ Embracing St. Bernard* is an even greater picture.

The latter was bought by the Prado in 1940, having been originally in the possession of the Carthusian Monastery of Porta

Coeli, near Valencia. Until some fifty years ago it was ascribed
to Zurbarán, but is now known to have been a product of the
last phase of Ribalta's life.

While much of Ribalta's best work is in Valencia this painting
in oils is the equal of anything from his brush, both for its masterly
sense of design and its sober employment of colour. The half-
length figure of the saint—his face alight with divine love, and
his right hand touching the arm of Jesus in a gesture of utter
content—is intensely moving. The ivory coloured habit, and rosy
flesh tints used in the painting of Our Lord, make it easy to
understand how this picture was first mistaken for the work of
Zurbarán.

The *St. Francis* was bought from the Capuchin monks of Valencia by King Charles IVth. in 1802, and appears in the first
Prado catalogue. Its unpretentious naturalness has always been the
object of favourable criticism, despite all changes in artistic taste.

The Dominican Friar Juan Bautista Maino, was born in Pastrana, and is completely identified with the Spanish School of painting
which immediately preceded the appearance of Velázquez. After
many years of indifference to his work the critics of today greatly
admire this artist. Perhaps the finest of Maino's canvases in the
Prado is that portraying *The Recovery of Bahia in Brazil.* Employ-
ing clear tones, the group on the left of the picture is surprisingly
modern in its conception, and the profile of a woman carrying
her naked child in her arms, is beautifully executed. In 1701 this
canvas was believed to be the work of a Flemish artist, and was
valued at 120 «doubloons». Looted by Napoleon's brother Joseph,
it returned to Spain in 1815, hanging first in the Academia de
San Fernando and, in 1827, in the Prado.

The Adoration of the Magi by the same artist strikes us as
being too vivid in its colouring but, if you can overlook this possible defect, it will be seen that both the Virgin and Child are
beautifully portrayed. *The Adoration* came from the Museo de la
Trinidad in 1873.

Opposite «El Españoleto's» pictures (Hall XXVI) there are
works by Zurbarán, which naturally encourages comparison between
these Spanish contemporaries.

Zurbarán's work was more placid than that of Ribera; his colouring clearer, and he does not share the latter's predilection for muscular nudes.

Zurbarán's reputation was at its lowest during the second half of the XIXth. century and, now that he is valued more highly the Prado has only an inadequate collection of his works. The two best—scenes from the life of St. Peter Nolasco—cannot he compared with those to be seen either in the Seville Gallery or in the Monastery of Guadalupe, and there is not a single example in the Prado of Zurbarán's famous series of portraits of monks, in which the artist's skill is most clearly revealed.

However, *The Visions of St. Peter Nolasco* and his *St. Casilda* are intensely Spanish in their sober and restrained treatment, perhaps even more so than the work of Velázquez, who travelled extensively in Italy whereas Zurbarán never left his native country and whose whole training and experience reflect his background. In any case the tendency to compare the two is unwise, as they should be judged separately on their own merits.

Zurbarán was a master of design, and a good, sober colourist. When the theme required it, however, as in the figure of St. Casilda, he knew how to vary his tones, though he obviously preferred white, grey, black and clay-coloured reds. His blues tend to be too dark, and his use of green and ochre unattractive.

The two signed canvases, *Visions of St. Peter Nolasco,* in the Prado were painted in 1629 for the Sevillian Convent of the Merced Calzada. By the beginning of the XIXth. century they were in the possession of the Sevillian collector, López Cepero, who presented them to King Ferdinand VIIth. in exchange for a copy of a Velázquez portrait.

It is believed that the beautiful *St. Casilda* was painted for an altar, but it was mentioned in the 1814 inventory of the Royal Palace in Madrid, and came to the Prado five years later.

The Prado possesses 10 canvases by Zurbarán which are not on exhibition. These include six of the famous *Hercules* series, painted to decorate the Salon de Reinos in the Retiro Palace, and are among the best of the artist's known work.

It was not until quite recent times that Friar Juan Andres Rizi's portrait of Don Tiburcio de Redin y Cruzat was definitely identified. As late as 1818 it was catalogued in the Royal Palace at Aranjuez as a representation of Hernán Cortés by Velázquez. In 1819 it was listed as a *Portrait of an Unknown Gentleman,* by Mazo, and it was only Don Aureliano de Beruete who finally ended the uncertainty.

Technically speaking it is the equal of anything from the brush of Velázquez, and strongly recalls that artist's portrait of Pulido Pareja in the National Gallery in London.

This portrait, together with that of Friar Alonso de San Vitores in Burgos, are the two best-known examples of Rizi's work.

The name of Antonio de Pereda is not as well-known as it should be, judging by the quality of his three signed canvases now before us, two of them on religious themes and one on an historical subject, and all intended for the Retiro Palace.

The historical picture was looted by the French General Sebastiani, at the same time as several by Rubens, from the Convent of Loeches, and for many years was believed to have been lost. However, it appeared at a sale in London in 1912, when it was bought by the Hungarian collector, Marced de Nemes, for the Prado.

In our opinion *St. Peter Freed by an Angel,* which was bought by the Prado in 1931 from the Count de Leyva, is a finer example of Pereda's work than his *St. Jerome,* and reveals the artist's unmistakable quality.

This section of the Gallery (Hall XXV) is completed by one portrait of King Philip IVth's first wife, Isabel de Bourbon, by an unknown artist.

José de Ribera—«El Españoleto» (Hall XXVI)—was born in Játiva, near Valencia, in 1591, but worked in Naples for most of his life. There are nine oil-paintings by him here, and others on the Ground Floor. Although Ribera lived amid the brilliant light and shade of the Mediterranean he chose only dark tones and sombre themes for his work, following in the Caravaggio tradition of «tenebrism». One critic wrote that he «painted everything by the light of the wine-cellar», and it is true that a large area of his canvases appear to be covered by impenetrable shadows which, however, serve to heighten the dramatic contrast offered by the small area of intense light in which the main interest of the picture is centred.

Ribera's style was particularly admired in Spain, as it broke away from the old Italian and Flemish tradition and opened up new ideas and theories in technique for the younger Spanish artists of his day, paving the way for Zurbarán, Velázquez and many others.

The essential quality of Ribera's work can be appreciated in the two oil-paintings exhibited here—*The Martyrdom of St. Bartholomew* and *The Dream of Jacob*. Here the criticism which applies to almost all painters, except Greco and Fra Angelico, immediately strikes us—namely, the entire absence of religious feeling in the figures portrayed. Ribera's Saints reveal no spiritual exaltation, being nothing more than a faithful portrait of the model. The religious theme, in fact, again serves only as a pretext for painting, and the Saints can often be identified only by some conventional attribute or device.

The Martyrdom of St. Bartholomew is beautifully balanced and executed but, alas, the Saint is all too obviously a typical Italian fisherman. The strong bodies of the three executioners, however, are almost worthy of Michael Angelo in their muscular splendour. This canvas is less dark than many by Ribera, who signed it not only with his name but also with the word «Spanish», as he frequently liked to do. It was painted in 1640 and entered the Prado from the Royal collection. In 1794 it was valued at 60.000 «reales».

The Dream of Jacob, also signed, belongs to the previous year, and is an impressive example of Ribera's work, the face of Jacob, and the dream of the ladder itself, being admirable. When it was in the Elizabeth Farnesio collection it was ascribed to Murillo. It came to the Prado from the Academia de San Fernando in 1827.

Isaac and Jacob, which is signed and dated 1637. It was valued at 24.000 «reales» in 1794, and came to the Prado from the Academia de San Fernando in 1827. Its extraordinarily rich and beautiful tones of red and blue are strongly reminiscent of the great Venetian Masters.

Ribera made three canvases of *Mary Magdalene* (some believe of St. Tháis) of which the one before us now is the best. Generally speaking Ribera was less successful in his portraits of women, but in this case the extraordinary beauty of the model—the same as was used for the *St. Agnes* in the Dresden Museum—is faithfully reproduced, and provides a striking contrast to contemporary Italian work which, by the early XVIIth. century, was already decadent.

Mary Magdalene was in the collection of the Marqués de los Llanos, before being catalogue in the new Royal Palace in Madrid in 1772.

Ribera's *The Trinity*, believed to have been painted in 1636, was bought for the Prado in 1820 by King Ferdinand VIIth. from his own Court Painter, Agustin Esteve. A duplicate is still in El Escorial, and is particularly notable for the vigorous modelling of the body of Christ.

HALLS XII, XIII, XIV AND XIV A

The Prado contains no less than 50 paintings by Velázquez, including the best by the Sevillian Master. No other Gallery in the world has such a collection, which includes examples from every phase of his career.

Leaving out all works in which the hand of a pupil can be detected, or concerning which there is the least possible doubt as to authenticity, there are the following pictures by Velázquez on exhibition here.

In Hall XII, *The Topers, The Spinners, The Surrender of Breda, The Forge of Vulcan, Mercury and Argus,* the figures of Aesop, Menipo and Mars, and 17 portraits. These last include five of King Philip IVth. and two of Prince Baltasar Carlos, besides those of the Princes Ferdinand and Charles, Queen Mariana of Austria, the Princess Margarita, the Duke of Olivares, the 10th. Count of Benavente, the sculptor Martínez Montañés, the court jesters and dwarfs Pablo de Valladolid, Barbarroja and Don Juan de Austria. This hall also contains a landscape by Mazo, entitled *View of Saragossa,* in which the figures in the foreground were painted by Velázquez.

In Hall XIII two *Crucifixions, The Adoration of the Magi,* portraits of Sister Jeronima de la Fuente, Don Diego de Corral, and

Doña Antonia de Ipeñarrieta, and two head and shoulders—one of which is believed to be a self-portrait: the second of the painter Francisco Pacheco.

In Halls XIV and XIV A there are religious pictures, *St. Anthony the Abbot with St. Paul the Hermit*, the *Coronation of the Virgin Mary*, two small landscapes of the Villa Medici; two small portraits—one of the Infanta Maria, and the other of Doña Juana Pacheco, wife of the painter—and five full length portraits of a jesters and dwarfs el Primo, Niño de Vallecas, Calabacillas, don Sebastián de Morra and the incorrectly entitled, *Don Antonio el inglés*, and Philip IVth. with a lion at his feet.

Next to Hall XIV, dominated by the equestrian portrait of Isabel de Bourbon, the picture *Las Meninas*—probably the most famous of all Velázquez's works—is exhibited alone in Hall XV.

In addition to the canvases already mentioned Halls XIII, XIV and XIV A also contain the following pictures: a landscape attributed to Velázquez entitled *The Arch of Titus in Rome*, another landscape by Mazo, *Philip IVth. and Mariana of Austria at Prayer*, and a portrait of Prince Carlos, in which the hand of one of Velázquez's disciples can be detected.

While the sculptor Rodin likened Velázquez to Phidias, there have been modern critics who expressed the opinion that he was too cold and academic to be considered really great. Such criticisms arise from the present day superficiality which, in its restless search for new forms of expression, cannot understand Velázquez's balanced harmony, proceeding from the serene and logical mind possible only to his day and age.

In fact, Velázquez was the natural product of his times. By the end of the XVIth. century the artistic revival of the Italian Renaissance had spent itself, the place of the great Masters being occupied by decadent copyists of mediocre talent. Their last really valuable ideas were assimilated by Greco and transplanted by him to Spain, where they were developed along new and highly individualistic lines. At this psychological moment Velázquez appeared on the scene, and may be said to have written that last chapter in the book of Renaissance painting which the Venetians were unable to complete.

This final flowering of Renaissance Art was simultaneously

reflected by Velázquez in Spain, and by Rembrandt, Van Dyck and Frans Hals in the Low Countries and, of these, Velázquez and Rembrandt are the supreme exponents. Velázquez was painting during the years when the baroque was in the ascendant, yet his work reveals no trace of its elaborate contortions. In fact, his delicate silver tones and deeper, but still subtle, browns and reds, supporting a design that deliberately eliminates all inessentials, contains the very essence of Andalusia transferred to the crisper air of Old Castile, the vigorous «chiaroscuro» of his youth gradually giving place to the delicate graduations of light and shade of his maturity.

Yet he is a supreme craftsman who masters every aspect of his art with brilliant certainty. True the early Velázquez is frankly experimental, but the mature artist is able to suggest a background of subtle light and shade never achieved by anyone else.

The three canvases in the Prado belonging to Velázquez's earliest Sevillian period, when the artist was about 20 years old, are *The Adoration of the Magi*; the portrait of Sister Jerónima de la Fuente, and that believed to be of Francisco Pacheco in Hall XIII. All reveal something of Ribera's strange predilection for darkness, but as soon as he reached Madrid Velázquez became a favourite at Court, and developed his own special genius for portraiture.

Inevitably his rapid rise to fame attracted jealousy, and the King himself told him that his rivals accused him of being able to paint nothing but heads. While this accusation was profoundly untrue, Velázquez's interest was undoubtedly centred in the portrayal of the human face, and it was in this that he achieved his greatest triumphs, capturing character, individuality and temperament as very few others have ever succeeded in doing.

Even before he reached Madrid Velázquez had made himself a complete master of his art, as he demonstrated in the brilliant study of Sister Jerónima. However, after his arrival at Court, he developed still further his extraordinary ability to record the essential qualities of even the most unattractive models.

The only type of Velázquez's work that is not represented in the Prado is of the female nude, of which only a single example is known to exist, namely that on exhibition in London. Apart from this it is extremely rich in portraits illustrating every phase of his career, the only outstanding portraits by Velázquez which are not to be found in the Prado being those of Pope Innocent Xth, the Infanta María Teresa, Prince Philip Prospero and Juan de Pareja. The rest are all here: King Philip IVth. and his two Queens; the King's brothers, Ferdinand and Charles, and his sister María; the King's son and daughter, Baltasar Charles and Margarita; his minister the Duke of Olivares, and also the King's numerous dwarfs and jesters. There are, additionally, the portraits of the lawyer Don Diego de Corral; the sculptor Martínez Montañés; of Ambrosio Spinola, and the Count of Benavente, and many others. Besides these there are portraits believed to be of the artist's wife; of his own Master, and a copy by Velázquez of a Góngora head, which is in the possession of the Prado. Finally, there is Velázquez's own self-portrait in middle age, which gazes back, serene but pensive, from the shadows of his masterpiece, *Las Meninas*.

The most notable of his works are now examined separately.

HALL XII

It is generally agreed that the most important of Velázquez's works, belonging to the period between his arrival in Madrid and his first visit to Italy, is that known as *The Topers*.

In 1629 King Philip IVth. paid the artist—who had already been appointed to the official position of Court Painter—the sum of 100 silver ducats for this canvas, and was so delighted with it that he forthwith decided to send Velázquez to Italy to complete his studies. *The Topers* appears in the catalogue of the old Alcazar Palace for the first time in 1636, the inventory of 1794 valuing it at 40.000 «reales», while that of only 40 years later estimated its worth at no less than 180.000 «reales».

The theme of *The Topers* is vaguely mythological, and was at one time known as *The Triumph of Bacchus*, and represents a group of riotous wine-bibbers, wreathing themselves with vine leaves. It is a brilliant portrayal of the high spirits engendered by a drunken orgy, but the moral warning is present in the two faces looking directly out from the canvas, upon which the characteristics of the habitual drunkard are unmistakably stamped. A baroque painter, equally with a modern one, would have felt obliged, in treating such a theme, to include various unpleasant details in the interests of «realism», but Velázquez contrives to give a certain dream-like elegance even to a scene which, in its essence, is fundamentally vulgar.

The Topers probably reveals the culminating point in Velázquez's technical development before he left Spain. His subsequent contacts with the works of the great Italian Masters inevitably influenced the next period of his life when, with maturity added to experience, he was finally to establish himself as a painter of permanent world repute.

From the period of Velázquez's first visit to Rome the Prado possesses his *Vulcan's Forge*, the artist's treatment of which shows that he was far more interested in executing a number of studies of the male nude than in the theme that the title suggests, and Italian influences are more pronounced in this canvas than in any other. Painted in 1630, it was brought to Spain by the artist and, 4 years later, was presented by Don Jerónimo de Villanueva to the King. First catalogued in the Retiro Palace in 1701, it was valued at 80.000 «reales» in 1794, and at exactly double that sum in 1834. The theme, which is presented with a certain element of satire, shows the appearance of Apollo, determined to revenge himself upon Venus for her refusal of his love by denouncing to Vulcan the whole tale of her misconduct with Mars.

The Surrender of Breda commemorates Philip IVth's great victory, when the Genoese Ambrosio Spinola, defeated the Dutch under Justin de Nassau. It was painted some time before April 1635, the capitulation itself having taken place 9 years earlier. Velázquez met Spinola during his first visit to Italy, but the Genoese leader had been dead for several years before the painting of *The Surrender of Breda*, as had also the Dutch leader, but the artist still contrived to present them both as vital, living personalities. The 30 spears or lances, appearing in the right upper section of the canvas, temporarily earned for it the title of *The Lances*. Incidentally, it is suggested that the soldier behind the horse on the extreme right may be a self-portrait of the artist.

In 1834 *The Surrender of Breda* was valued at two million «reales», and many people consider it the finest work of Velázquez's second period—1630 till 1646—and second only to *The*

Topers among all that he painted before the age of 35, and it certainly provides a marked contrast to the crude colouring used in such early work as *The Adoration of the Magi*. In fact, the period of time which separated the painting of *The Adoration of the Magi* and *The Surrender of Breda* is 16 years, while that between *The Surrender of Breda* and another of his greatest works, *The Spinners*, is 22 years.

The Spinners is believed to have been painted in 1657, that is to say, one year after Velázquez finished his supreme masterpiece *Las Meninas*, so that it is clear that this is the period in which the artist reached the summit of his powers. The room shown in the background is the Madrid tapestry works in St. Isabel Street, and shows five of the workers engaged in their craft.

Originally the property of Don Pedro de Arce, Master of the Hunt at the Court of King Philip IVth, it was hung in the old Alcázar de Madrid, being damaged during the great fire of 1734. Removed to the Retiro, and thence to the new Royal Palace, it was valued at 60.000 «reales» in 1794. By 1834, having already reached the Prado, the estimate of its value had doubled but, even so, it was still, strangely enough, considered less than half as valuable as Juan de Juanes' *Last Supper*.

In *The Spinners*—as in *Las Meninas*—Velázquez clearly sought to interpret the very essence of light and shade, and those indefinable qualities of depth peculiar to an interior. In this he is the antithesis of the Flemish primitives. While, for example, the Master of Flémalle, in his *St. Barbara*, depicts every detail with meticulous care, Velázquez seems to see his subject through half-closed eyes, that record only the essential qualities of the individual and his surrounding. In some strange way he makes un feel that it is the background alone that lends significance to the human figures that he portrays.

It is often essential for a work of art to be seen from a distance, and this is particularly true of Velázquez. From close at hand it is possible to perceive only a series of heavy blobs of colour yet, from the correct distance, these resolve themselves into living human figures of an intense vitality. The extraordinary subtlety of the artist is fully revealed by the fact that the most arresting figure in the whole canvas is a young peasant girl, her face hidden, barefoot and poorly dressed, whose only adornments are the bright ribband in her hair and the simple bracelet on her left wrist.

It is interesting to reflect that, in his 58th year, the Master turned away from the recognized beauties of the Court, to the portrayal of whom he had devoted the best part of his life, and sought his inspiration among the simple people who had been his models when he was a young and unknown artist in his native Seville. In any case it cannot be denied that in these working women of the Madrid tapestry factory Velázquez found the material for his greatest works, and it was his representation of such simple and unglamorous types, and in a setting devoid of all adornment, that he finally demonstrated the range of his genius.

It is perhaps permissible to wonder how many masterpieces have been lost through the failure of other artists to find this inspiration in the every day people surrounding them. Most of the great Masters of each century have devoted themselves exclusively either to religious themes or to fashionable portraiture, but if, instead, their brushes had recorded the colourful life of XVIth. and XVII th. century Spain the world of today might be richer by innumerable canvases such as «The Spinners».

Velázquez was the first to break away from convention, but he did so only after he had recorded the decadent splendours of the Court of *Philip the Great*, where Royalty was encouraged to squander the hours of its youth in producing such elaborate coiffures as those shown in the portraits of Queen Mariana and the Infanta Margarita.

Velázquez made several portraits of his patron the Duke of Olivares, among them the equestrian one painted in 1634 which is on exhibition here in Hall XII. It clearly reveals the strict instructions given by the Duke as to the way in which he wished to be presented to posterity, and the result, as might be expected, lacks something which the artist would otherwise have imparted to it.

From its original owner this somewhat idealized portrait passed into the possession of the Marqués de la Ensenada, being bought by King Charles IIIrd. for 12.000 «reales» in 1769. After its entry into the Prado, in 1834, it was valued at 80.000 «reales».

The portrait of the Andalusian sculptor Martínez Montañés was formerly believed to be of Velázquez's friend Alonso Cano. Supposedly painted in 1637, when the sculptor visited Madrid to model a statue of King Philip, it was catalogued among the Royal collection at the Quinta del Duque del Arco and, in 1834, was valued at 10.000 «reales». Considered by many to be among the best of the Velázquez's portraits in the Prado, the head and right hand reveal the artist's unmistakable technique. Strangely enough the left hand was never finished.

The half-length portrait of the Count of Benavente was in the collection of Queen Elizabeth Farnese, where it was mistakenly ascribed to Titian. It came to the Prado in 1819, and was valued at 16.000 «reales» in 1834. The influence of Greco, as well as of Titian, are easily discernible, but both colour and design are in Velázquez's best vein.

This Hall contains various portraits of King Philip IVth. and his family, including Queen Mariana, the Infantes Don Carlos and Don Fernando, Prince Balthasar Carlos, and the Infanta Margarita. The three of the King show Philip, first as a severe young man dressed in mourning and was painted in 1628; the second, on horseback, which is even earlier in date and was intended for the Salon de Reinos in the Retiro Palace; and the third, in hunting costume carrying a gun and with a sporting dog at his side, which is dated as between 1635 and 1638.

The equestrian portrait is additionally interesting as including by far the most successful representation of a horse ever achieved by Velázquez, whose animals were not, as a rule, very convincing. There is a charming group of King Philip, Don Fernando and Balthasar Carlos, believed to have been intended for the Royal Hunting Lodge at La Torre de la Parada which, however, does not appear in the Catalogue until 1701. In 1834 those of the King and his son were valued at 40.000 and 25.000 «reales» respectively.

The three full-length portraits are made against a background of stormy sky and grey countryside, and are brilliantly executed, though it is the exquisite profile of the young Prince beneath his gaily coloured cap that most clearly reveals the hand of a

Master. Velázquez painted several portraits of the young Heir
to the Throne, who was to die before reaching manhood, of which
this, and another on horseback, are to be seen in the Prado. This
equestrian portrait was valued at 50.000 «reales» in 1834. The
Prince's pony has been the object of much adverse criticism, and
its preposterous barrel-like belly is surprising in the work of an
artist usually so scrupulous in his attention to detail One explanation of this improbable-looking steed is that Velázquez intended
the portrait to be hung high above a certain door in the Palace,
and seen thus from below its proportions are immediately restored
to normal.

Although Velázquez's name is associated with the portraiture
of royalty he never lost his interest in depicting the strange
characters that helped to make up the Court of a XVIIth. century
monarch. Among these were the macabre collection of jesters and
dwarfs with which Philip IVth. liked to surround himself. To any
one possessing the insight into character of a great portraitist it
was clear that these figures of fun were anything but gay, and
only one of the many inhabitants of this strange half-world painted by Velázquez is portrayed laughing. The exception is in the
portrait of Calabacillas, and even here the idiotic merriment so
brilliantly portrayed moves us more to pity than to amusement.
Velázquez, in 10 portraits, reveals two distinct kinds of Court
Jester, the buffoons and the dwarfs. Among these there is a further
division between the sane and the obviously cretin. Pablillos, Barbarroja and Don Juan de Austria appear to have been physically
normal, while the dwarfs El Primo, Morra, Don Antonio el Inglés,
Mari Bárbola and Nicolás Pertusato are at least sane. Clearly
abnormal, both physically and mentally, are El Niño de Vallecas
and Calabacillas. Incidentally, both the dwarfs Mari Bárbola and
Nicolás Pertusato appear in the supreme Velázquez masterpiece,
Las Meninas.
The artist's preference for full-length portraits of his models
standing is clearly revealed, in that all this motley crew of Court
Jesters are so presented. They were painted at various dates between 1633 and 1644; that of Pablo, being the earliest of the
series, and that of Calabacillas, El Niño de Vallecas and Barbarroja dating from three years later. The richly coloured portrait

of Don Sebastián de Morra is attributed to the year 1643 or 1644. Uncertainty surrounds the date when Velázquez made his portrait of Don Juan de Austria, and it is certain that the lunatic Don Antonio el Inglés had died in 1617, before the artist first left Seville.

All Velázquez portraits of Philip IVth's Court Jesters were in the Royal collection, and those of Pablo de Valladolid, Barbarroja and Don Juan de Austria were in the San Fernando Academy from 1816 until 1827, when they were sent to the Prado. The first Prado Catalogue included those of Morra, Don Antonio el Inglés, El Primo, El Niño de Vallecas and Calabacillas. By 1834 each was valued at 20.000 «reales».

Which is the best of this strange set of portraits? Probably those of Don Juan de Austria and El Niño de Vallecas, the latter being a masterly study of character.

The Prado possesses two Velázquez portraits of Queen Mariana of Austria, the niece and second wife of King Philip IVth. One has been in the Louvre since 1941, as part of an exchange of works of art between France and Spain; the other and, in our opinion, the better, being catalogued Number 1191. Some critics believe that the canvas lent to the Louvre is only a copy of that now on exhibition in the Prado, though Señor Sánchez Cantón holds that they are duplicates, both by Velázquez, though that in Paris was the earlier, and painted from life. His view is supported by the greater freedom of style displayed in the Prado canvas. Although this portrait is not so fine as that of the Infanta Margarita, there is a striking similarity of treatment. Both mother and daughter are wearing the hooped skirts typical of the period, and are similarly coifed with a large feather head-dress, while both hold a white gauze handkerchief across their wide dresses.

Queen Mariana was an unattractive model, heavy and unintelligent, in marked contrast to her beautiful predecessor Isabel de Bourbon. It required all the Master's genius to make something of interest from the sullen expression and stiff artificiality of his subject, but somehow he overcame even these handicaps, and the result is technically brilliant.

This portrait belongs to the last period of Velázquez's life, being ascribed to the years 1652-53, and reached the Prado from El Escorial in 1845.

That of the Infanta Margarita is believed to have been Veláz-quez's last portrait, and some critics are of the opinion that it was finished by Mazo after the Master's death in 1660, and there are undoubtedly signs of another brush in the treatment of the model's face, neck and hands, as well as in the background, though the hair, dress and handkerchief are unmistakably by Velázquez.

The portrait of Queen Mariana is a study in black, silver-grey, pale red and ochre, while that of the Infanta is an equally mar-vellous symphony in red and silver, picked out with white and gold. Both reveal the supreme phase in the artist's development, his characteristic restraint in the use of heavy colour, and his inimitable delicacy of touch. The portrait of the Infanta Margarita came to the Prado in 1834, when it was valued at 30.000 «reales».

Velázquez's *Mercury and Argus* was painted between the years 1657 and 1659 as one of a series of mythological themes for the Mirror Salon in the old Alcázar de Madrid. Three were destroyed in the great fire of 1734—*Venus and Adonis, Apollo Chastizing a Satyr* and *Psyche and Cupid;* while *Mercury and Argus* reached the Prado in 1834, when it was valued at 30.000 «reales».

Modern critics consider it one of the less notable of Veláz-quez's canvases, being over-dark but, even so, it is a fine example of the artist's technique during the last years of his life.

Two figures by Velázquez, entitled *Aesop* and *Menipo,* which have been in the Prado since 1819, were painted in 1639 and 1640. Valued at 25.000 «reales» each in 1834, they were intended for the Torre de la Parada. They are impressions of the famous author of the fables, and the cynic philosopher Menipo—the expression of the latter being particularly clever.

The canvas, *View of Saragossa,* is catalogued as being by Veláz-quez and Mazo—the small figures in the foreground by the for-mer, and the landscape by the latter.

HALL XIII

The Adoration of the Magi was painted in Seville in either 1619 or 1617, and is the earliest known work by Velázquez, who must have been only 18 or 20 years old at the time. The Virgin

Vista del Jardín de la Villa Médicis.
Jardín de la Villa Médicis.

View of the Garden of Villa Medici.
Gärten der Villa Medicis.

Las Hilanderas (fragmento).
Les Fileuses (détail).

The Spinners (detail).
Die Spinnerinnen (fragment).

Las Meninas.

La Reina María de Médicis.　　　　Queen Mary of Medici.
La Reine Marie de Médicis.　　　Königin Maria von Medici.

RUBENS

Las tres Gracias.   The Three Graces.
Les trois Grâces.   Die drei Grazien

RUBENS

Danza de aldeanos.   Peasant Dance.
Danse des paysans   Der Bauerntanz

RUBENS

El Jardin del Amor.
Le Jardin de l'amour.

The Garden of Love.
Der Garten der Liebe.

La Piedad.
La Piété.

Piety.
Die Kreuzabnahme.

La coronación de espinas.   The Crown of Thorns.
Le couronnement d'épines.   Die Dornenkrönung.

Retrato de Paul de Pont (?) (fragmento).
Portrait de Paul de Pont (?) (détail).
Portrait of Paul de Pont (?) (detail).
Bildnis von Paul de Pont (?) (fragment).

La familia del pintor.
La famille du peintre.

Jordaens'Family.
Die Familie des Malers.

JORDAENS

Meleagro y Atalanta.
Méléagre et Atalante.

Meleager and Atalanta.
Meleager und Atalante.

PAUL DE VOS

Cacería de corzos.
Chasse de chevreuils.

Hunting-party.
Hirschjagd.

Artemisa. Artemis.
Artémise. Artemis.

Concierto rústico. Rustic Concert.
Concert rustique. Laendliches Konzert.

VAN UTRECHT

Filopémenes, descubierto.
Philopoeman découvert.

The discovery of Philopemenes.
Der ertappte Philopemenis.

Mary is believed to have been a portrait of his wife, while his father-in-law served as model for one of the Wise Men of the East. Some critics have even suggested that the face of the youngest is a self-portrait of the artist in his youth. This picture, when in the Escorial collection, was ascribed to Zurbarán owing to the dark background so characteristic of that artist.

The full-length portrait of Jerónima de la Fuente is signed and dated 1620, but was only rediscovered as a genuine Veláz-quez in 1927, when it was shown in Madrid at a Franciscan Art Exhibition. It came from the Convent of St. Isabel in Toledo, and was bought for the Prado in 1944. There is a duplicate in Madrid in the possession of Señor Fernández Araoz.

Next comes the portrait of Don Diego de Corral, Judge of the Supreme Court of Castile, with his wife, Doña Antonia de Ipeñarrieta and their small son, painted in Madrid in about 1631. Incidentally, Don Diego was the only Judge who opposed the imposition of the death sentence in the famous trial of Don Ro-drigo Calderón. Some critics claim that the unconvincing treat-ment of the child suggests that it was not the exclusive work of Velázquez. This canvas was the property of the Dukes of Villa-hermosa, and was patriotically presented to the Prado by the late Duchess in 1905, after she had refused various large offers from a foreign collector.

The chief point of interest in this picture is the head of Don Diego, which reveals a perfection of technique not to be found elsewhere until a later period in the artist's life.

Velázquez's *Crucifixion* is of special interest because of its total absence of the traditional emphasis upon physical agony. In it the body does not seem to hang from the Cross but rather to rest upon it, and nowhere is the smooth flow of its majestic lines bro-ken by the contortions that are the usual indication of suffering. The bowed head is hidden by the hair, and the body reveals its dreadful punishment only by the small wound in the side, and the thin threads of blood on hands and feet, and the whole im-pression, while intensely moving, is strangely serene and peaceful.

The Crucifixion was painted between 1632 and 1635 for the Madrid Convent of San Plácido, and came to the Prado in 1829.

It became the joint property of the Infante Don Luis, the Countess of Chinchón and the Duke of San Fernando de Quiroga. The Countess took it with her to Paris where, in 1826, it was valued at 20.000 francs. However, the Spanish Government intervened to buy it for 30.000 «reales», but the Countess died before the sale was completed, and her heirs refused to be bound by the unratified agreement. Fortunately for Spain the Countess in her Will bequeathed the right to her brother-in-law, the Duke of San Fernando de Quiroga, to select for himself any one picture from her collection, and he chose Velázquez's *Crucifixion*, later presenting it to King Ferdinand VIIth. In 1834 it was valued at 120.000 «reales».

The story is that *The Crucifixion* was commissioned by King Philip IVth. as a gift to the Convent of San Plácido in order to persuade the Abbess to permit him to visit a beautiful nun named Margarita, with whom he was passionately in love. The story rings true from what we know of King Philip IVth. and of this particular convent, but Madrazo preferred to suggest that the picture was presented to the Convent by its Patron, Don Jerónimo de Villanueva.

There are many *Crucifixion* in the Prado painted by great Masters, but this by Velázquez is almost certainly the finest. Don Antonio Ponz, when he saw it late in the XVIIIth. century, still in the possession of the Convent said, «It is the most powerful, yet delicate of studies, coloured with all the astonishing richness of Velázquez's palette».

The small sketch, *Christ on the Cross* may have been a preliminary design, for approval by the Convent of San Plácido, before Velázquez began work on his *Crucifixion*. It is particularly interesting for the fact that, although both signed and dated 1631, it was discovered only a few years ago in the Madrid Convent of the Bernardas del Sacramento. As a token of their gratitude for the rebuilding of their Convent, which was destroyed during the Civil War, the nuns then made a gift of the sketch to the Government, who presented it to the Prado in 1946. It was very unusual for Velázquez to sign his works—this sketch, and his portrait of the nun Jerónima de la Fuente, being the only examples of his signature among the 50 undisputed examples in the possession of the Prado.

Two early portraits—one of Francisco Pacheco and the other a possible self-portrait—reveal a vigorous «chiaroscuro» treatment, together with a wonderfully exact technique. The former, believed to have been painted in 1619, was catalogued among King Philip Vth.'s collection at La Granja in 1746. The supposed self-portrait is ascribed to the year 1622-1623.

HALLS XIV AND XIV A

Halls XIV and XIV A also contain examples of Velázquez s work, though in his less interesting capacity as a painter of landscapes and religious themes.

The Coronation of the Virgin Mary, for example, finely depicts a beautiful girl, but both she and the figures by her side are far more human than divine. In short Velázquez, being by nature a genius of portraiture, always portrayed mythological or religious characters, without any of the essential idealization of the human models he engaged. *The Coronation* is believed to have been painted about the year 1642 for the Queen's Chapel, reaching the Prado in 1819, and being valued, 15 years later, at 80.000 «reales».

Velázquez's fondness for painting landscapes is further revealed in the large canvas, *St. Anthony the Abbot and the Hermit St. Paul*, and by the two small sketches of the Villa Medici.

Although the theme of the former is of St. Anthony marvelling at the Raven which every day brought bread to the Hermit in his grotto it is, in fact, a large landscape, filled with rocks, trees, and distant mountains set against a clouded sky.

Velázquez's two sketches of the gardens of the Villa Medici in Rome immediately call to mind the «impressionists» of the late XIXth. century. Formerly it was believed that these sketches belonged to the artist's first visit to Italy, but today the technique they reveal is taken as proof that they were painted during his second visit. They were both in the inventory of the Alcázar Palace made at the time of the death of King Philip IVth.

The portraits of Philip IVth's sister, Doña María de Austria, and that believed to be of Doña Juana Pacheco, are both fine pictures. The former was painted in Naples in 1630, but was still in Velázquez's studio when he died 30 years later, while the other, believed to have been painted two or three years later, was bought by Queen Elizabeth Farnese. Since 1746 it has been catalogued as a *Portrait of the Artist's Wife.*

The head and shoulders portrait of King Philip IVth. numbered 1185, was painted during the last 5 years of the artist's life, and the King, already over 50, is shown in a plain black suit and starched ruff against a dark background. His calm, but haunted, heavy face and pale hair, are portrayed with all the impressive simplicity of which Velázquez was the master.

Some years ago there was a controversy as to whether or not the portrait of a dwarf, erroneously entitled *Don Antonio el Inglés,* was painted by Velázquez—Allende-Salazar asserting that it was from the brush of Carreño. The technique is strongly reminiscent of Velázquez, and the official Prado Catalogue continues to attribute it to him on the grounds that certain parts of the canvas are undeniably by the Master, while the name of his collaborator, if any, is not known.

Portraits and landscapes by Juan Bautista del Mazo reveal why Velázquez's son-in-law was also his favourite pupil. His works, however, seem to suggest that he suffered from, rather than profited by, his close association with his great master, and his portraits are in so exact an imitation of Velázquez's style as often to make them indistinguishable.

HALL XV

The picture which is generally accepted as being Velázquez's greatest masterpiece is exhibited alone in this small hall, with a mirror on the opposite wall so that the visitor may appreciate its extraordinary depth and perspective with the heightened clarity sometimes provided more effectively by a reflection than by the reality itself. This is the world-famous *Las Meninas*—the Maids of Honour. Its setting is the studio of the official Court Painter.

and it shows the King and Queen reflected in a mirror in the background, Velázquez himself at his easel, the little Princess Margarita, her two young Maids of Honour, two of the Court dwarfs and a dog. Behind the main group are two secondary figures, and also that of a man in the far background, framed in the doorway as though looking back at the moment of his departure.

Las Meninas was finished in 1656, four years before Velázquez's death, and was greatly appreciated by the King who, two years later, rewarded the artist with the Knighthood of Santiago. After Velázquez's death the Cross of the Order was painted on to the tunic of his self-portrait in *Las Meninas* at the personal order of the King. *Las Meninas* was saved from the 1734 fire which destroyed the old Alcázar de Madrid Palace, and the slight damage that it then received skilfully repaired by Don Juan García de Miranda. In 1794 it was valued at 60.000 «reales».

Most people agree that it was Velázquez's culminating triumph, and many believe that it is the greatest picture by any artist to be seen in the Prado. Unquestionably it is one of the finest in the entire world, if only for its almost uncanny mastery of interior lighting, and it aroused Gautier to write, «This is Nature itself imprisoned within the bounds of realism». Weisbach summed it up as «the image of a whole epoch, surpassing the boundaries of mere portraiture». As early as the XVIIth century Lucca Giordano said of *Las Meninas*, «It is the very Theology of Painting».

It is of interest to recall that although the Dutch and Flemish schools had already produced masterly «interiors», they had never been successfully attempted anywhere else until the time of Velázquez.

The beautiful grouping of the figures leaves nothing to be desired, but the sense of life and movement, together with the technical mastery of colour and tone, combine to make us realise that we are in the presence of something that has been achieved very seldom in the history of art, seeming to invite us to join the courtier group that still awaits us there, living and moving, across the gulf of nearly 300 years.

The effect is not so much «impressionistic» as of a magically induced illusion, by which we are permitted briefly to share in the lives of the Royal Family, and the scope of Velázquez's genius can be very simply understood by comparing this courtly scene with his equally brilliant handling of the simple workers in *The Spinners*.

In *The Spinners* the interest is deliberately focussed upon one figure, but in *Las Meninas* this is not the case, the eye being equally attracted to four—the Maid of Honour, Doña María Agustina Sarmiento, the little Infanta, the second Maid of Honour, Doña Isabel de Velasco, and the dwarf Mari-Bárbola. But it is not long before it is drawn irresistibly to the artist's face, the graceful gesture of Nicolasito Pertusato, and to the sleeping dog on the right.

Velázquez portrayed, as no one else could have done, the tragic dignity of King Philip IVth's decadent Court, shadowed by some occult foreknowledge that only one more King of the Austrian House would ascend the Throne of Spain—the great line of the Emperor Charles Vth. petering out in near-madness just 44 years after *Las Meninas* was painted.

FLEMISH PAINTERS

After having seen *Las Meninas,* and before returning to the Central Gallery, it is convenient to visit the halls containing over 160 pictures by Rubens, his pupils and copyists.

Peter Paul Rubens—the outstanding figure of XVIIth. century Flemish art—was born 22 years before Velázquez, that is to say in 1577. He visited Spain twice on official diplomatic missions, in 1603 and 1628, and on the second occasion is known to have met the young artist from Seville, going with him to look at some paintings.

Rubens was already at the height of his fame, but does not appear to have exerted any influence on the 29 year old Spaniard who, by this time, had already decided for himself the style he intended to pursue.

The huge canvas *The Adoration of the Magi,* with its brilliant colours, is typical of the work of Rubens, as are also his *Garden of Love, The Three Graces, Nymphs and Satyrs* and *The Judgment of Paris*. Additionally, there is the remarkably fine portrait of Mary of Medici, Queen of France and mother-in-law of the Spanish King Philip IVth.

Rubens is the supreme exponent of the baroque, but reflection makes it clear that all the works attributed to him in the world's art galleries could not possibly have been painted by one man alone, and reason suggests that often he acted as an artistic director to his disciples and pupils rather than as the actual painter. His studio was specially equipped for this kind of work, which was so well done that it is often impossible to be certain which sections of any canvas were the Master's own work, and which were painted, under his direction, by one or more of his collaborators.

However, in thirteen cases in the Prado collection, it has been possible definitely to identify his assistants, who are listed in the catalogue as having been Paul Bril, Van Dyck, Van Uden, Paul de Vos, Snyders (two) Jan Brueghel (three) and Van Tulden (four).

There are no less than 67 ascribed to Rubens alone, even though some of these also reveal the work of another hand, though in a less marked degree. There are also three copies by Rubens from the originals by Titian and Holbein.

There are works by Rubens in Halls XVI, XVII, XVIII, XVIII A, XIX and XX, and also on the Ground Floor of the Prado. As the Flemish School was so very prolific in its output we shall confine ourselves here to a description of a few of the most important examples.

HALL XVI

This is devoted entirely to Rubens.

The religious scenes of *The Adoration of the Magi*, the *Piety*, *The Pilgrims of Emmaus* and the *Holy Family with Saint Anne*, alternate here with the compositions of *Adam and Eve* (this is a copy of the painting by Titian of the same title, already seen in Hall IX), and *St. George and the Dragon*, as well as the equestrian portraits of Philip IInd. and the Cardenal Infante Don Fernando and the twelve figures of the Apostolate.

The Adoration of the Magi is impressive for its rich colouring as much as for its great size. Even in this theme Rubens was unable to restrain his predilection for painting massive or muscular nudes, and the first impression is that he gave more attention to the powerful figures carrying their gifts to the Child than to the

Child Himself. It was painted for Antwerp Town Hall in 1609. Three years later it was presented to Don Rodrigo Calderón, as a reward to the Minister for his labours on behalf of Spain and, on his death, was bought by King Philip IVth. It is believed that Rubens added to the original canvas during his second visit to Spain in 1628.

The Holy Family seems almost too tranquil a subject to have appealed to such an enthusiastically pagan painter as Rubens, but his representation of the Child is most attractive, though his Virgin Mary is the conventional Flemish type, and totally lacking in any suggestion of spirituality.

The Master's vigorous style and warm colouring are unmistakably in evidence in this canvas, which came to the Prado from El Escorial in 1839, having been bought from the sale of its original owner, the Marqués del Carpio, at the end of the XVIIth. century.

Here we may see the most powerful of all Rubens's religious paintings, which is called *Piety*. It belongs to the artist's last epoch, and was bought by King Philip IVth. From El Escorial it came to the Prado in 1837. The face of Christ is of a moving nobility, and the drawing of His naked body is masterly.

Rubens' baroque style is fully revealed in the equestrian portraits of King Philip IInd. and, even more so, in that of the Cardinal Prince Ferdinand, younger brother of Philip IVth. and is strongly marked in the dynamic figure of *St. George* in his *St. George and the Dragon*.

HALL XVI ᴀ

This is devoted to Van Dyck. The Prado possesses 7 Van Dycks based upon religious subjects, one on a mythological theme and 15 portraits.

Van Dyck, who was a disciple of Rubens, is one of the outstanding portrait painters of the XVIIth. century, and his likeness of the Marchioness of Leganés rivals the work of his great contemporary Velázquez. He lacked Holbein's exactitude of design, but had a more controlled sense of line than Rubens, and his title to greatness is now generally admitted. Unfortunately the lack of English portraits in the Prado prevents us from tracing the tremendous influence that Van Dyck, as Court painter to King

Charles Ist. of England, undoubtedly exercised upon the brilliant British portraitists of the XVIIIth. century, such as Gainsborough and Reynolds.

In the Hall are two portraits of women and 10 of men, including a self-portrait together with Van Dyck's friend Sir Endimion Porter. This oval canvas, which is considered one of his best, was the property of Queen Elizabeth Farnesio, and was catalogued at the Palace of La Granja in 1750.

Other interesting portraits are those believed to be of the engraver Paul du Pont, the musician Jacob Gaultier, painted in 1635 and 1625 respectively; that of the armless painter Martin Rickaert, and of Count Henri de Bergh, finished in 1630.

Fromentin commented: «If we examine Van Dyck's portraits in detail we see that the Master is at his best in whatever aspect of his subject happened specially to interest him, such as an idle hand, the turn of a woman's wrist, or a slender be-ringed finger. His style owes nothing to the XVIth. century, belonging wholly to the new generation of the XVIIth. century, whose full development he never lived to see. He showed a greater interest in the textures of silk and steel and in the fashions of his day than can be found in any of Rubens' work though, like his Master, he is occasionally guilty of a rather showy and mannered style in his efforts to create an impression of richness.»

The Arrest of Jesus belongs to Van Dyck's earliest years. It was bought at the sale following the death of Rubens for 1.200 Florins. In our opinion, Van Dyck's *Crown of Thorns* is a greater picture than his *Arrest of Jesus*, to which reference has already been made, and is probably his best religious work in the Prado. The rich and shining colours, and masterly sense of design, leave no doubt in the mind of the beholder that this is a great picture. Van Dyck presented it to Rubens and, at the sale following the latter's death, it was bought by King Philip IVth., reaching the Prado in 1839 from El Escorial. The Berlin Art Museum possesses a duplicate, which contains certain minor differences from the canvas now before us.

HALL XVII

This Hall contains pictures by Rubens, Catherine Ykens and Christian Luycks.

Mary de Medici is the best Rubens portrait in the Prado. Painted between 1622 and 1625 it was bought at the sale following his death in 1640. Also in the artist's best tradition is that of another Queen of France, the Spanish born Anne of Austria, wife of Louis XIIIth.

HALL XVII A

This Hall contains seven paintings by Jacob Jordaens, of which three are outstanding—a portrait group, a religious study, and the artist's rendering of a mythological theme. Additionally, there is a small sketch of exceptional interest to which we would like to draw attention.

The first picture, entitled *The Artist and his Family in a Garden,* is believed to have been painted in 1622, and shows us Jordaens, his wife, his daughter Elizabeth and a maid-servant. It was in the Royal Collection at Aranjuez in 1794.

The canvas known as *The Mystic Betrothal of St. Catherine of Alexandria* is believed by some critics not to be by Jordaens, but to be the work of Van Dyck and, when in the possession of Queen Elizabeth Farnesio during the XVIIIth. century, it was ascribed to Rubens. It also came to the Prado from the Royal Palace at Aranjuez.

Meleager and Atalanta, catalogued at the same time as the other two already mentioned, is really two separate canvases painted at different periods of Jordaens' life, though the junction was so skilfully made as to be invisible. The left half of the picture belongs unmistakably to the last period of the artist's life.

Lastly, there is the sketch mentioned above, showing the head and shoulders of three wandering minstrels, which some critics have attributed to Van Dyck.

Jordaens was a disciple of Rubens, but lacked the Master's powerfull sense of drama. Reinach said of him, «Jordaens is a brilliant painter but lacking in taste, occasionally producing a ralther ordinary imitation of Rubens».

The Prado contains none of Jordaens most typical canvases, though his *Meleager and Atalanta* gives a fair indication of his best style. His *St. Catherine*, though less brilliant, is technically remarkable, and his family group is beautifully composed and executed.

The sketch of the wandering minstrels seems completely modern in its vital realism.

The portrait of Doña Policena Spinola, Marchioness of Leganés, daughter of the victor of the Battle of Breda, is believed to have been painted when the artist Van Dyck was only 25, and is a feat which even Velázquez could scarcely have achieved at so early an age. Already the artist's special talent for the portrayal of hands is fully revealed.

HALLS XVIII AND XVIII A

The Garden of Love was bought by King Philip IVth. at the sale of Rubens work which followed the artist's death in 1640. In this canvas all the pagan elements beloved by Rubens are present—languishing, if over-nourished, ladies; pink and equally plump Cupids; ardent and muscular males; playing fountains, arrows, flowers and wine—combining to produce a scene of slightly turgid gaiety unimaginable to any Spanish artist of the same period, but one which nevertheless strongly appealed to the sensuous Philip IVth.

It is believed that King Philip IVth., personally commissioned Rubens to paint his *Perseus and Andromeda* which, however, was unfinished at the artist's death. Fortunately, Jordaens completed the canvas in such a clever imitation of the Master's style that it is difficult to distinguish which part is by Rubens and which by his successor. The model for the nude figure of Andromeda was almost certainly Rubens' second wife Helena Fourment, who is also recognisable as Venus in another work of Rubens' later years, *The Judgment of Paris*. Philip's younger brother, the Cardinal, wrote of *The Judgment of Paris* to the King, «it is Rubens' best work, the only criticism being that the three goddesses seem to be excessively naked».

The Prado contains many representations of mythological themes from the brush of Rubens, mention having already been made of *The Judgment of Paris, Perseus and Andromeda, Diana and Calixto,* and *Atalanta and Meleager.* Now we are before his *Rape of Ganymede, Ceres and Two Nymphs* and *The Three Graces.* Later we shall be seeing his *Birth of the Milky Way, Diana the Huntress, The Banquet of Tereo, The Rape of Hipodemia, Mercury and Argus,* and *Achilles.* However, although so numerous, none is the equal of the three naked figures representing the Graces—that on the left, incidentally, being Rubens' wife Helena Fourment.

The Three Graces was painted during the last years of the artist's life, and was kept by his wife in her bedroom after his death, ultimately being bought by King Philip IVth. One critic judged it the supreme example of baroque painting, writing «Rubens has here given us his ideal of feminine beauty—fleshy, pagan, sensual and gay—as typified by his wife Helena, who is the arch-type of the Flemish Venus now to be seen in every major European art gallery». The same writer, Díez Canedo, adds, «it is no accident that there are so many examples of Rubens' painting of mythological themes in the Prado, as a number were directly commissioned to decorate the Torre de la Parada in El Pardo just outside Madrid, where Velázquez was also similarly engaged. While our rich heritage of Titian is due to Philip IInd., we must equally acknowledge our debt to Philip IVth. when Spain was at her greatest, and Titian the supreme exponent of the art of his time, so both Rubens and Philip IVth. represented the last flowering of a vanishing age. From his early studies Rubens absorbed the best of the heritage left by the Italian Renaissance, and combined it with the essential elements found in the Flemish «primitives».

HALLS XIX, XX AND XXI

In Hall XIX are the pictures by Rubens known under the name of «Triumphs».

These «triumphs» belong to a series of 17 panels ordered from Rubens by the Infanta Isabel Clara Eugenia as designs for a tapestry for the Madrid Convent of Descalzas Reales. The artist completed the commission in 1628 for a fee of 30.000 florins. The «cartoons» for the tapestry to be manufactured in Flandes were completed simultaneously.

The panels were presented to Don Luis Méndez de Haro, and were bought for the Royal Collection in 1694 from his son.

Of the 8 possessed by the Prado the 3 best are to be seen in this Hall. Because of their relatively small size many people overlook them, though they are very well worth a more careful examination.

In Hall XX it is worth mentioning the painting entitled *Diana the Huntress*, in which it is believed that the dogs were painted by Paul de Vos, an artist who specialised in animal painting. Two large composition of this type, *Deer hunt* and *Deer brought to bay by hounds*, both in Hall XXI, bear witness to de Vos's mastery of this subject.

Here there are further examples of the rather showy Rubens School originating not only in Flanders, but also from the studios of the Master's Italian imitators. For the most part they do not merit more than a passing glance from the visitor, unless, of course, he is making a special study of the period.

HALLS XXII AND XXIII

This contains the best Dutch paintings possessed by the Prado, with works by Rembrandt, Gabriel Metsu, Adriaen van Ostade, Hobbema, Gerard van Honthorts, Grebber, Wouvermann, Schalcken, Potter, Koeninck, Ruysdael, Mierevelt, Coosemas, Palamedes and Brekelencam.

Rembrandt's *Artemis, Queen of Pergamo*—though doubt exists as to the model's identity—is signed and dated 1634, when the artist was only 28 years old. Some critics believe that the face is that of Rembrandt's beautiful wife Saskia, of whom he painted several portraits. First the property of the Marqués de la Ensenada, it was bought for 2.500 «reales» by King Charles IIIrd. in 1769. It is generally considered the best of Rembrandt's early works, and the ash-blonde hair, the pale hands and rich dress, backed by the vase in which, tradition asserts, the Leyden artist's ashes were presented to the Queen, is all in the Master's finest manner. There is also here Rembrandt's famous self-portrait, made when he was about 55 years old, which was bought by the Prado in 1944.

The four small signed oil-paintings by Van Ostade were bought by Charles IVth., and reveal the King's excellent taste.

Gabriel Metsu's *The Dead Cock*, also bought by King Charles IVth. is remarkable for its exquisite finish and detail, and the landscape by Hobbema, bought by the Prado in 1944, possesses a certain poetic quality. Van Honthorst's *Doubting Thomas* is not one of the artist's best works.

The Philosopher, signed by Salomon Köninck, is an exquisite example of the Dutch school. The Museum acquired this painting in December 1952.

Another beautiful canvas is the *Portrait of a Gentleman*, by Mierevelt, which boasts a very finished technique.

> In order to preserve historical sequence which we have so far followed we recommend the visitor to return to Hall XIII and the Gallery. In the connecting corridor he will pass four mythological works, two by Ribera representing the torments of Ixion and Ticio, and two by Titian on the punishments of Ticio and Sisifus. Additionally there are several pieces of sculptury, and a copy of Lucca Giordano's «The Death of Absalom» by Corrado Giaquinto. The original is at the Royal Palace at Aranjuez, and served as the model for the Royal Madrid Tapestry Factory, which produced one of its finest works from it in 1760.

The two Ribera canvases form part of a series of four painted in 1632, of which the other two—*Sisifus* and *Tantalus*—have been lost. Before reaching Spain the *Ticio* was on exhibition im Amsterdam when, according to Palomino, it produced so profound an impression upon a certain young matron that it caused her «to miscarry of a monster». These large male figures are fine examples of Ribera's deep knowledge of anatomy, but those by Titian are dark and without great interest.

> The central part of the Gallery forms a kind of «tribune» where there is a bust of Villanueva, the architect of the Prado. Below it is a tablet stating that, when the work of restoration was completed on December 12th. 1927, it was dedicated as an exhibition of Spanish painting. Beneath this is a bronze bust of the Emperor Charles Vth. by Pompeo Leoni, flanked by the equestrian portraits of King Philip IIIrd. and his Queen, Margaret of Austria. These equestrian portraits were painted by an unknown artist for the Salon de Reinos in the Retiro Palace, and reveal signs of having been retouched by Velázquez.
> Opposite, and on either side of the door leading to the Velázquez Hall, are landscapes by Velázquez and Mazo.

CENTRAL GALLERY

SECTIONS XXVIII AND XXIX

Here there are 13 works by Murillo on exhibition, including two large canvases in the form of arches, portraying the foundation of the Church of Santa Maria Maggiore; three versions of the *Immaculate Conception,* one of which was the favourite of Napoleon's Marshal Soult; three child studies entitled *The Children of the Shell, St. John the Baptist,* and *The Good Shepherd;* his rendering of the religious themes, *St. Bernard's Vision of the Virgin Mary, The Descent of the Virgin to reward St. Ildefonso* and, finally, the painting *St. Augustin.* Additionally there is a portrait of an unknown man, and a landscape of less importance.

Bartolomé Esteban Murillo was born in Seville in 1617, and, until recent times, enjoyed a reputation equal to that of his contemporary and fellow-townsman Velázquez. Today, owing to a change in taste, he is infinitely less admired than his great rival,

but there are many who still consider his religious paintings
unsurpassed. His most pitiless critics are the admirers of El Greco's
«psychological» portraits who, not unnaturally, can see nothing
of merit in Murillo's rich but conventional studies of nothing but
the outward aspect of his subjects.

In our opinion, Murillo is well worthy of study for his technical brilliance alone. The succession of rather sickly-sweet Virgins,
blond angels and cherubic children may easily lead to his vigorous
and finished workmanship being overlooked. While his brush
delighted in soft, feminine, or childish forms, his presentation of
them was always decisive.

It must be borne in mind that the themes which Murillo chose
to paint required rich colouring and gentle personalities, but there
is no lack of virility in the artist's handling of his subjects. Murillo's soft realism marks one of the highest points in Spanish art,
his essentially Iberian style being enriched by a close study of
Van Dyck, and he profoundly influenced the Sevillian School of
the XVIIth. century, as can be seen not only in the Prado, but
also, if the visitor wishes, in the Art Gallery of Seville. Many of
Murillo's paintings now in the Prado were brought from his native
Seville during the XVIIIth. century, and it is recorded that, when
on a visit there in 1729, Queen Elizabeth Farnesio, who was an
enthusiastic collector of Murillo's paintings, bought all she could
find. Among her purchases now in the Prado are, *The Holy
Family (del Pajarito), The Good Shepherd, St. John the Baptist,
The Children of the Shell, The Crucifixion, St. Anne and the Virgin Mary, The Annunciation, St. Bernard's vision of the Virgin
Mary, The Descent of the Virgin to reward St. Ildefonso, St. Francis of Paula, St. Jerome, Rebeca and Eleazar, The Old Spinner,
The Galician Woman* and an *Immaculate Conception*—this last
catalogued No. 973.

Murillo's three child portraits exhibited here would alone be
enough to establish his right to be considered a great painter,
his treatment of the delicate flesh tints in his *Infant Christ* and
St. John being exquisite, proving him Velázquez's equal at least
in this respect, whatever his detractors may say of his over idealization of smiling and beautiful children.

The two magnificent canvases depicting *The Foundation of
the Church of St. Maria Maggiore* were painted in 1665 for the

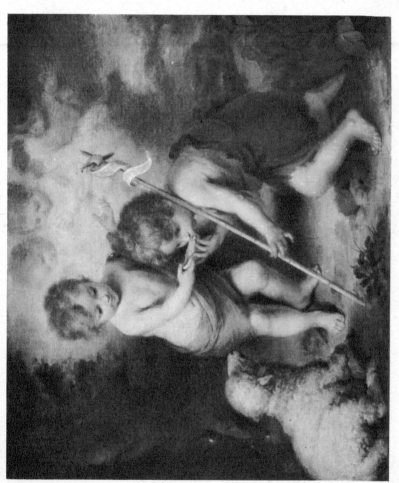

Los Niños de la concha.
Les Enfants à la coquille.

The Children of the Shell.
Die Kinder mit der Muschel.

La Inmaculada Concepción «de Soult».
Immaculée Conception «de Soult».
The Soult's Immaculate Conception.
Die unbefleckte Empfängnis «von Soult».

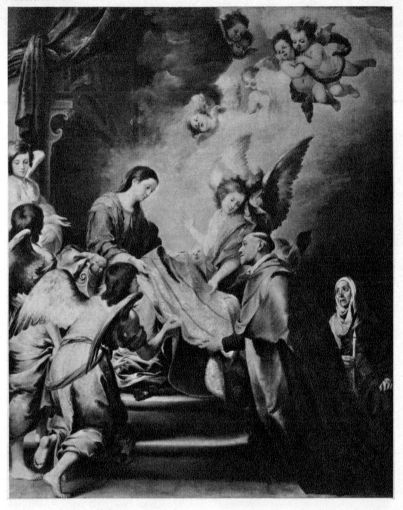

La Descensión de la Virgen para premiar a S. Ildefonso.
La Descente de la Vièrge pour récompenser Saint Ildéfonse.
The Descent of the Virgin to reward St. Ildefonso.
Die heilige Jungfrau steigt vom Himmel hernieder um den heiligen Ildefonsus.

El milagro del pozo.   The Miracle of the Well.
Le miracle du puits.   Das Wunder des Brunnens.

La Asunción.   The Assumption.
L'Assomption.   Die Himmelfahrt.

El Triunfo de S. Hermenegildo.
Le Triomphe de Saint Herménégilde.

The Triumph of St. Hermenegildo.
Der Triumph von Sankt Hermenegildo.

JOSE ANTOLINEZ

El tránsito de la Magdalena.   The Death of Mary Magdalene.
La mort de la Madeleine.   Der Tod Maria Magdalenas.

Juegos de niños.
Jeux d'enfants.

Children at Play.
Kinderspiele.

El Triunfo de San Agustín. The Triumph of St. Augustin.
Le Triomphe de Saint Augustin. Der Triumph von Sankt Augustin.

GOYA

La maja desnuda.

GOYA

La familia de Carlos IV.   The Family of Charles IV.
La famille de Charles IV.   Die Familie Karls des IV.

Retrato de Francisco Bayeu.   Portrait of Francis Bayeu.
Portrait de François Bayeu.   Bildnis von Franz Bayeu.

El Rey Felipe V de España.   The King Philip V of Spain.
Le Roi Philippe V d'Espagne.   König Philipp der V von Spanien.

VAN LOO

La familia de Felipe V.   The Family of Philip V.
La familia Philipp V.   Die Familie Philipps V.

POUSSIN

El Parnaso.   The Parnassus.
Le Parnasse.   Der Parnassus.

GUERCINO

Susana y los viejos.
Suzanne et les vieillards.

Susanna and the Elders.
Susanne und die Greise.

Seville Church of St. Maria la Blanca, from whence they were looted by Marshal Soult for Napoleon's collection. However, they were returned to Spain in 1815, being in the Academia de San Fernando until they reached the Prado in 1901.

The Patrician's Dream is particularly fine, the two sleeping figures and the rich golden tones employed by the artist placing it among his best works.

The better of the *Immaculate Conceptions* is, in our opinion, that which also attracted the artistically rapacious Marshal Soult. It was painted for the Hospital de los Venerables Sacerdotes of Seville, from whence it was taken to France, for sale by its «owner» to the French Government for 615.300 francs in 1852, and was then on exhibition in the Louvre Gallery for 90 years, where its exquisite modelling and rich colouring attracted world interest.

The full-length portrait known as *The Knight of the Collar* was bought in 1941 by the Prado from the heirs of the collector Don Tomás de Veri, and belongs to the last phase of Murillo's life, when his genius as a portraitist was fully developed.

The preoccupation with religious themes of Spain's XVIth. and XVIIth. century painters seriously limited their development in other directions, and this applies especially to Murillo, whose realistic genius as a portraitist alone raises his religious pictures above the contemporary level.

Murillo's tendency to handle a religious subject as a «genre» painting is clearly revealed in *The Descent of the Virgin Mary to reward St. Ildefonso* and *St. Bernard's Vision of the Virgin Mary*, which compare with his *St. Thomas of Villanueva*, or *St. Anthony* and the *St. Elizabeth of Hungary* to be seen in Seville. These first two canvases have been in the Prado since its foundation, and in 1794 were valued at 7.000 «reales» each.

In the opinion of Madrazo both belong to Murillo's best period, which fell between 1665 and 1682.

> The remainder of the Central Gallery contains, on one side, various religious paintings by Claudio Coello and Mateo Cerezo, on the other, there are canvases by Herrera («el Mozo»), José Antolínez, Villavicencio, Alonso Cano, Escalante and Carreño.

The position of Claudio Coello in Spanish art, at a moment when foreign influences were particularly strong, is of special interest. Coello died at 51, and was the outstanding artist during the reign of the last of the Spanish Hapsburg Kings, Charles IInd. It is said that the arrival in Madrid of the Neapolitan artist Lucca Giordano in 1692 hastened his death.

The best of Coello's works in the Prado are his *Triumph of St. Augustin, Virgin and Child surrounded by Virtues and Saints,* and *Virgin and Child worshiped by St. Louis, King of France.* All three are signed, and the first two dated, respectively, 1664 and 1669. The third of those mentioned above belonged to the Marqués de la Ensenada, from whom it passed into the possession of King Charles IIIrd., before reaching the Prado in 1819.

The Triumph of St. Augustin was painted for the Augustin Monastery of Alcalá de Henares, and reached the Prado from the Museo de la Trinidad. It is a typical Spanish baroque triptych of the late XVIIth. century in which, however, can be traced the influences of Velázquez, Murillo and Rubens.

After the death of Velázquez Spanish art became more ornate, gradually degenerating into the over-complex, decorative style known as baroque. Pedro de Madrazo said of Claudio Coello, «He was a colourist in the tradition of Rubens and Veronese». We do not ourselves share the view that he successfully combined in himself the best of Cano's design, Murillo's use of colour and Velázquez's understanding of perspective, but he possessed a genuine quality of his own, more essentially Venetian than Flemish in its inspiration. He is notable, in a period of general Spanish decadence, as being the last Spanish artist in the great tradition until the emergence, nearly a century later, of the tremendous figure of Goya.

Mateo Cerezo, who died aged 40 in 1666, has had a number of canvases in the Prado since 1819, the best of which are his *Assumption;* the *Mystic Betrothal of St. Catherine,* dated 1660 and bought by King Ferdinand VIIth. in 1829, and *St. Augustin,* signed and dated 1663, which was bought by the Prado in 1926. While overshadowed by his contemporaries, in this golden age of Spanish art, he reveals a certain mastery in his handling of colour which suggests that, if he had lived longer, he might have achieved real greatness.

Another painter, who was more famous for the richness of his palette than for his accurate drawing, was José Antolínez. The Prado contains two of his altar-pieces, *The Immaculate Conception* (Hall LXXIV) and *The Assumption of Mary Magdalene*. Both reveal how Titian still actively influenced the Madrilenian School of the late XVIIth. century.

The Assumption of Mary Magdalene—the better of the two in our opinion—was bought by King Ferdinand VIIth. in 1829 for 2.500 pesetas, under the impression that it was by Mateo Cerezo.

The Triumph of St. Hermenegildo, by the Seville artist Herrera (the Younger), was originally the property of the Carmelite Order, from whom it was bought by King Ferdinand VIIth. for 10.000 «reales» in 1832.

Posterity does not endorse Herrera's high opinion of himself, and he is chiefly remembered as the spiteful rival of Coello, Cerezo, Antolínez and Cabezalero, though this particular canvas of his reveals an undoubted impressionistic talent.

Children at Play, by the Andalusian knight, Don Pedro Núñez de Villavicencio (1644-1700), is an attractive study, in the style of Murillo, of typical street urchins of the period. It is of special interest as a portrayal of life in the XVIIth. century, at a time when most other contemporary artists were more concerned with religious themes than with their own times. It was catalogued in the old Alcazar Palace of Madrid in 1686 though, at that time, it was a smaller canvas than that which is on exhibition today, being subsequently enlarged by Lucca Giordano. It is almost the only signed work by Villavicencio in existence, and so has a certain value apart from its obvious intrinsic worth.

The Miracle of the Well, by Alonso Cano, represents an episode in the life of St. Isidro, and came into the possession of the Prado in 1941. The origin and history of this picture are unknown, but we shall have more to say of Cano when visiting the Ground Floor.

On either side of the painting of Herrera *(The Younger)*, we see the portraits of Queen Mariana, widow of Philip IVth., and of

King Charles IInd., his son; both are by Carreño, and are painted in the «severe style» which is a characteristic of this master. The portrait of the Duke of Pastrana is also the work of this artist, but shows more elegance of style, with a slight influence of Van Dyck. It was acquired for the Museum in 1896, at the sale of the House of Osuna, and the price paid was 15.000 pesetas.

HALL XXXII

We are now in the presence of the last and, in the opinion of many, the greatest exponent of Spanish art: Don Francisco Goya y Lucientes.

The Prado contains the following canvases by Goya: two group portraits *(Charles IVth. and his family* and the *Osuna Family)*; three equestrian portraits of Charles IVth., Queen María Luisa and General Palafox; nine full-length portraits of King Charles IIrd, Charles IVth, Queen María Luisa, Ferdinand VIIth. the Marchioness of Villafranca, the Duke of Alba, General Urrutia, Doña Tadea Arias de Enríquez and of Cardinal Luis de Bourbon. There are also nine half-length portraits of Josefa and Francisco Bayeu (Goya's wife and brother-in-law), General Ricardos, King Charles IVth, Queen María Luisa, the Marchioness of Villafranca, the actor Máiquez, Don Manuel Silvela and Don Juan Muguiro. Additionally there are the head and shoulders self-portrait; another of Van der Gotten, and the two famous «majas»: the nude and the clothed; there are the head and shoulders self-portrait; another of Van der *The Fight in the Puerta del Sol,* and the terrifyingly realistic *Moncloa Executions.*

There are also no less than 46 canvases designed for the St. Barbara Tapestry Works; 14 more with the strange, haunted designs with which the artist chose to decorate his own home; three oval canvases representing Agriculture, Industry and Commerce; two landscapes entitled *La pradera de San Isidro* and *The Hermitage of San Isidro,* the *Crucifixion,* the *Holy Family;* the sketch *St. Justa and St. Rufina,* and three still-life studies.

Lastly, there are 7 studies entitled *The Milk-maid of Bordeaux, Blind Man's Buff, The Drunken Builder, The Cut-throat,*

The Bonfire. Un garrochista and *The Exorcised One*, besides a «caprice» known as *The Colossus*.

It is a tremendous collection, and one from which it is possible to form a really comprehensive idea of the vital, many sided personality of Goya, though there is reason to suppose that it will be still further increased in the near future by legacies and purchases. Already it is the finest Goya exhibition in existence and, in our opinion, it would be better if nothing a later date were permitted in the Prado, subsequent artists belonging elsewhere, since they play no part in the great pageant of European Art developing between the late XVth. and early XIXth. centuries.

Probably the most famous canvases by Goya in the Prado are *King Charles IVth. and his Family*, the two *Majas*, and his portrait of his brother-in-law Bayeu. The two religious paintings are of small interest.

Goya's designs for the Royal Tapestry Works only occasionally reveal the artist's authentic genius, as he was severely limited by the requirements of his employers. There are more of these to be seen on the Ground Floor of the Prado, to which we shall refer later.

When the Prado was restored, and partially rebuilt through the generosity of the Duchess of Parcent, in 1927, the circular hall at the end of the Central Gallery was intended for the exhibition of the best of Murillo's works, but it has actually been devoted to Goya's two «majas» and some of his most notable portraits.

Immediately facing the visitor upon entry is his *Charles IVth. and Family* while, flanking the door, are the world famous *Naked Maja* and *Robed Maja*. Here there are also the equestrian portraits of King Charles IVth. and of Queen María Luisa, both of which appeared in the first Prado catalogue. Additionally, there are a number of other portraits, and some preliminary sketches for his masterpiece *King Charles IVth. and his Family*.

King Charles IVth. and his Family reveals Goya as a superb colourist, though the general composition of the picture is not particularly inspired. Nevertheless, it is considered one of the three greatest treasures in the possession of the Prado, the other two being Velázquez' *Las Meninas*, and Jordaens' *The Artist's Family*.

King Charles IVth. and his Family contains the portrait of 14

persons, if we include the little boy in arms, and a self-portrait
of Goya himself in the background. It was painted in the Royal
Palace at Aranjuez in 1800, and 39 years later entered the Prado,
being then valued at 80.000 «reales». Unfortunately, the canvas is
showing signs of deterioration.

The tendency to compare this with *Las Meninas* is hardly justified, Velázquez's masterpiece being technically the superior from
almost every point of view.

Although Goya was more interested in portraying women than
men the Prado does not contain a single female portrait by him
in his best vein. Probably that of Doña Tadea Arias de Enríquez
with its fine grey tones and pale rose background, is the best
to be seen here. It was presented to the Prado by the grandsons
of Doña Tadea in 1896. Of the equestrian portraits that of Queen
María Luisa is outstanding, and it is interesting to recall that only
three «sittings» were required by the artist in order to complete it.

The half-length portrait of an unknown woman, catalogued
No. 722, unfortunately shows clear signs of having been folded into
four before it reached the Prado from the Museo de la Trinidad
in 1866.

Goya himself considered his portrait of Manuel Silvela, painted during the years of the French occupation, to be one of his
best, both in its colouring and design. It was bought by the Prado
in 1931.

The large portrait of General Urrutia, painted some time
during the last decade of the XVIIIth. century. It was bought for
50.000 pesetas in 1896 at the sale of the collection of the Duke of
Osuna, and is an example of the artist's best style.

His portrait of his brother-in-law Francisco Bayeu, was made
in 1795—the year of his model's death—and there is another in
the Valencia Art Gallery. This portrait was exhibited, unfinished,
in the Academia de San Fernando in the following year and,
in 1866, it was bought for 400 «escudos» on behalf of the Museo
de la Trinidad. It reached the Prado in 1872. This particular canvas
is often referred to as «a symphony in grey», and is accepted as
one of Goya's finest portraits, even though it had to be completed
from a self-portrait made by the dead artist.

Goya achieved his effects either with a rapid, and almost impressionistic simplicity or, alternatively, by a totally contrasting extreme attention to detail. This portrait of Bayeu, together with his naked «maja», are the most striking examples of his second technique.

Of Goya's many paintings of «majas», the two on exhibition near the entrance to this hall are the most famous, perhaps because of the widely held belief that the model was the beautiful Duchess of Alba, and the legend that she was the artist's mistress. The two paintings are identical in pose, the sole difference being that one is nude and the other clothed. One popular explanation of the two versions of the same pose is that the Duke of Alba suddenly expressed a desire to see for himself exactly what kind of portrait of his wife the artist was painting. Strongly suspecting that the Duke would not approve of the nude study, which was already finished Goya, working at top speed, completed the other, modestly robed one, just in time to satisfy the suspicious husband. The story is the more credible as Goya, on occasions, could work at almost unbelievable speed. Additionally, the head of the robed «maja» is obviously a copy from the other one, and the dress itself also shows signs of having been painted in haste.

However, the official catalogue discounts these romantic stories, and states that the Duchess of Alba was definitely not the model for either these portraits.

The two «majas» vere painted between 1797 and 1798 and, in 1808, were the property of Queen María Luisa's favourite and Minister Manuel Godoy, who also owned the only other Spanish female nude of which we have record, namely Velázquez's *Venus of the Mirror*. The naked «maja» was at one time in danger of being burned as indecent, but was hidden in the Academia de San Fernando, and entered the Prado in 1901.

Much has been written about Goya's «majas», from the technical as well as the romantic point of view. Señor Sotomayorr has recently pointed out, with truth, that the head of the nude «maja» is badly set upon the shoulders. Generally speaking the nude is the more finished work of the two, the clothed figure revealing a quite different, and far more impressionistic, technique.

CORRIDORS

The corridor which encircles the main Goya Hall, and is numbered XXXI, contains a number of very fine pictures by Maella, Meléndez, Esteve, Carnicero, Amiconi, Panini, Bayeu, Corrado Giaquinto, Giovanni Domenico Tiepolo, Vicente López and some by French painters.

The works of most interest and artistic value to be found in these passages are those of Tiepolo and Giaquinto. This Neapolitan, who worked in Madrid for nine years (1753-1762) left some admirable paintings here that influenced the artistic formation of our painter Goya. The large-scale, beautiful allegory entitled *Justice and Peace*, the religious scenes of *The Prayer in the Garden* and *The Descent from the Cross* and the compositions *The Sacrifice of Iphigenia* and *The Battle of Clavijo* bear witness in the Prado to the great artistic merit of Corrado Giaquinto.

Antonio Carnicero's curious picture *The Ascent of a Montgolfier Balloon in Madrid*, painted at some date between 1780 and 1790, is interesting for the glimpse it provides us of contemporary fashions. It was bought for 3.000 pesetas at the 1896 auction of Osuna House.

There is a discreet *Portrait of an Unknown Lady* by the same artist, which formed part of the Bosch legacy to the Prado, which was also, for some time, ascribed to Goya.

We have here a portrait of a girl, signed by Agustín Esteve, a disciple of Goya, which is full of charm and interest.

The Prado contains many still-life pictures by Luis Eugenio Meléndez of which some are on exhibition here. Meléndez, who was sometimes called «the Spanish Chardin», usually initialled all his canvases, and those before us were painted at various dates during the late XVIIIth. century for the Royal Palace at Aranjuez. They are realistic and carefully executed, though uninspired.

Giovanni Domenico Tiepolo, who was in Madrid in 1772, painted a series of eight canvases for the Church of St. Philip Neri on the following themes: *The Garden of Gethsemane, The Scourging of Jesus ,The Crown of Thorns, The Fall on the Road to Calvary, The Casting of lots for Christ's Raiment, The Crucifixion, The Descent from the Cross,* and *The Burial of Christ.*

The predominant tones are of varying grey, but the composition reveals a certain mastery of design. Those on exhibition here are *The Fall, The Casting of lots* and *The Burial,* the other five of the series being on the 2nd Floor of the Prado. In our opinion, the series should not be divided up in this way, but be shown together as they formerly were in the Museo de la Trinidad.

Giovanni Domenico was the son of the famous decorator Giovanni Battista, of whose work we shall have something to say in reviewing the contents of the next hall.

HALL XXXIII

The portrait of Louis XVIth. by Antoine Callet is in the approved manner for display in a Royal Gallery, and was a gift from the tragic French King to the Count of Aranda. It gives the unfortunate impression that Louis' corpulent figure was only, with difficulty, restrained within the bonds of his magnificent clothes!

HALLS XXXIV, XXXV AND XXXVI

FRENCH PAINTERS

The Prado does not contain anything like so representative a collection of French paintings as it has of Spanish, Italian and Flemish works. Those that it does contain, by Poussin, Watteau and Claude de Lorraine, not to mention lesser artists, will not bear comparison with the pictures to be seen here from the other three great Schools.

Señor Sánchez Cantón, who has written a small guide book to the French pictures in the Prado, claims that they are the least frequented of any the building, and adds, «This may be because French classical art was under the influence of Rome and Bologna, where as the Spanish school were inspired by the far greater Flemish and Venetian painters. French artists were primarily concerned with faithfully portraying their subject, while the Spanish are more interested in depicting the human emotions. French painters favoured mythological themes, at a time when this kind of work was unknown in Spain, and they also specialized in landscapes in which the centre of interest was some man-made building, while in Spain they were concerned only with untouched nature. Similarly, while Spanish portraiture was essentially sober and realistic, that of France was frankly superficial. Again, the manner with which the artists of the two countries treated religious subjects is fundamentally different.»

«To understand French painting, therefore, it is necessary to realize that it belonged to another fashion and style, in which the artist's objectives were accuracy of design, the balance of the composition as a whole, the display of classical erudition and refinement, and the presentation of erotic themes.»

Any visitor entering this Hall XXXIV will be immediately struck by the large canvas entitled *The Family of King Philip Vth.*, which was painted in 1743 by Louis Michel Van Loo.

Despite its faults this picture is interesting as providing a typical example of French art of the period, and in demonstrating the influences at work upon Spanish painting in the lean years before the emergence of Goya. To understand how complete was this period of decadence in Spanish art, it is only necessary to compare Van Loo's *The Family of King Philip Vth.*, and Velázquez's *Las Meninas*, separated in time by only 87 years, but by a whole age in terms of quality. The simplicity, dignity and genuine greatness of Velázquez's art had been replaced by the cold superficiality, the affected conventionality, of such as Van Loo.

Designed to occupy the wall of a Royal Palace, its pictorial merits satisfied the limited artistic requirements of the period, and it is perhaps unfair to compare its slick, studied, and fundamentally false elegance with the work of the giants of the preceeding century.

Placed upon an easel opposite Van Loo's *Family of King Philip Vth.* is a delicately coloured portrait of Louis Ist, at about the age of 10. He was to be King of Spain for a few months in 1724 during a stormy interlude in the reign of his father, Philip Vth. It is ascribed to Houasse (1680-1730) who lived in Madrid for some years, and was clearly influenced by Velázquez.

The portrait of Louis XIVth. the Roi-Soleil of France, is by Hyacinthe Rigaud (Hall XXXV), and displays the usual preoccupation of the French Court Painters of the period, namely to please their sovereign rather than to achieve a great work of art. Showy and conventional, it presents Louis XIVth. as he wished to be remembered by posterity, rather than as a human being.

Rigaud (1659-1743) painted this portrait during the first decade of the XVIIIth. century, and it belonged to Louis' grandson, King Philip Vth. of Spain, entering the Prado in 1827. It is believed that the background is by Parrocel.

The French artist Nicolas Poussin was a contemporary of Velázquez, and it has been said of him that he was to the art of his times much what Racine was to its literature. Both were classicists rather than classic: learned lovers of the antique, studious, but uninspired; interested in the form, but politely ignorant of the spiritual substance of what they were portraying.

Poussin is the supreme example of the academic neo-classicism of the period. Trained in Rome and inspired by Raphael, his two dark canvases, *The Bacchanal* and *Parnassus*, painted at the same time as Velázquez's *The Topers*, give a very fair idea of his capabilities.

Sánchez Cantón, writing of these two pictures says, «*The Parnassus* is inspired by Raphael's Vatican Stanzie fresco, into which he has introduced certain baroque elements. The nude figure of Castalia is the main difference between the two, while the ghosts flying among the trees reveal the influence of Titian. Calliope, the Muse crowning the Poet, is simply a copy of Minerva, without the usual helmet and spear. The other conventional figures shown are presumably intended to portray Dante, Petrarch and Aristotle on the right, and Homer, Virgil and Horace on the left. The colouring, particularly the yellows and blues, is more attractive than was usually the case with Poussin».

He continues, «*The Bacchanal* reveals the «*Philosopher Painter*»

in a rather more inspirational vein, and is superior to the
Bacchanals ordered by Cardinal Richelieu. It shows Bacchus invit-
ing Ariadne and Cupid to mount his panther-drawn carriage. Before
them goes Silenus, mounted on an ass, and various dancing bacchantes. The best group is that on the right of the canvas, showing
a naked and drunken bacchante, riding a deer and supported by
a satyr and a goat-footed child».

In our opinion, Poussin's *Meleager's Hunting Party* is the best
picture by the French master in the possession of the Prado. His
St. Cecilia, also on exhibition here, belongs to the same period
as the other three paintings by him specially mentioned and com-
pletes a representative collection of his work.

The exquisite French painter Antoine Watteau died when he
was only 37, but was the dominating figure among the contemporary school composed of Poussin, Le Brun, Fragonard, and the
landscape painter Claude Gellée. There are two oil-paintings by
Watteau in this hall, entitled *Country Dance* and *The Gallant Feast,*
which were once in the Elizabeth Farnesio collection. They are
excellent examples of the «boudoir» pictures which portray life
during this greatest century of French history.

Pierre Mignard is another of the French artists with a notable
piece of work hung here.

The landscapes of Claude de Lorraine, with rather dark colours,
are most characteristic of the art of this famous master.

The work of Simon Vouet shown here is exquisite, and the
composition dynamic, with clear, gay colouring.

HALLS. XXXVII AND XXXVIII

In these two Halls are exhibited several paintings by Italian
artists. In our opinion, the most notable of these are those painted
by the Genoese Giovanni Benedetto Castiglione (called «il Gre-
chetto»), the Bolognese Francesco Giovanni Barbieri (known as
«il Guercino»), Danielle Crespi, Francesco Furini and Guido Reni.

Castiglione was a painter whose fame is inferior to his merit,
as is the case with so many artists. His works, generally carried out

in warm colours, show a solid technique, sure drawing and a careful execution. The scene of *Elephants in the Circus* is brilliantly composed, and the movement harmonious. His *Diogenes*, a signed painting which belonged to the collection of the painter Maratti, from whose legacy it was acquired by King Philip Vth., is also most impressive in its composition.

The painting by Furini entitled *Lot and his daughters*, with its beautiful nude figures, is an important work.

The painting by «Guercino» *Susanna and the Elders*, painted at the height of the artist's powers (he was born in 1591), is considered to be his chief work, and was executed under the influence of Caravaggio. It originally decorated the royal apartments in the Monastery of Escorial.

The *Piety*, a work signed by Crespi, was acquired for the royal collection in the sale of paintings which had belonged to the Marqués del Carpio. The nude figure of Christ is superbly modelled.

The *St. Sebastian*, by Guido Reni, was formerly in the collection of Isabel Farnesio. It is an excellent painting, attractively executed.

HALL XXXIX

The Venetian Giovanni Battista Tiepolo, who died in 1770, shares this hall with Luis Paret y Alcázar, born in the same year as Goya, and the Valencian portraitist Vicente López Portaña (1772-1850), who succeeded Goya as official painter to the Court of Spain.

Tiepolo spent the last eight years of his life in Spain, and several of the richly coloured ceilings in the Royal Palace in Madrid are his work. His oil-paintings in the Prado, however, cannot be compared with the fresco decorations, where his baroque technique had greater scope.

His best works here are the fragments transferred from the walls of the Church of St. Pascual in Aranjuez, painted in 1769. They were removed to make way for some much inferior work by Mengs.

The most notable examples of Tiepolo's art to be seen here are his *Immaculate Conception, St. Pascual Baylon, St. Francis of Assisi, Angel Bearing the Eucharist, Abraham* and *St. Antonia de Padua,* the first and third of which are signed.

The Immaculate Conception first appears in the Prado catalogue of 1828, and the canvas *St. Francis* was discovered, rolled up and broken, as late as 1914. The outstanding merit of Tiepolo was his brilliant handling of colour, which clearly reveals his Venetian birth and training.

There are 7 signed pictures in the Prado by Luis Paret—5 in this hall, and two more on the second floor—and all possess the same attractive sense of atmosphere, though perhaps his *King Charles IIIrd. Dining in State* is the most notable. The artist signed this with the quaint phrase, written in Greek characters, «Luis Paret, the son of his father and his mother, painted this». This canvas was for many years in Rusia, and was bought in 1933 from funds bequeathed to the Prado by the Count of Cartagena. Paret's small *Masked Ball,* unknown until then, was bought with the same funds in 1944.

Luis Paret received less attention from the critics than he deserves, being a gifted colourist who achieved many original effects. He was a man of great personal culture, and has sometimes been called «the Spanish Watteau».

Probably because he was able to travel widely throughout Europe, Paret managed to avoid the mannerisms of the period, and his small groups of figures, dominated by his special shades of blue, are often exquisite.

The Valencian Court painter, Vicente López Portaña, has a number of not very remarkable portraits on exhibition here, and also a fresco, painted in 1818 for the ceiling of the small palace, known as the *Casino de la Reina,* that was presented by the city of Madrid to King Ferdinand VIIth's second wife, Isabella de Braganza. It was sent to the Prado in 1865.

López was an excellent designer, but tended to overburden his canvases with detail. However, unlike such great portraitists as Holbein and Dürer, who also delighted in detail, the Spanish painter reveals no corresponding perception of character, preferring to model his style on Mengs rather than Goya. His ten portraits on exhibition here reveal him as little more than a painstaking artisan; whose whole talent seems to have been devoted to the portrayal of clothes, lace, feathers and embroidery, rather than to the human subject of the portraits.

The best of his works, in our opinion, is his portrait of Goya, in which there are indications that his model intervened to prevent López's excessive attention to detail. However, that of Queen María Cristina de Bourbon—and particularly her dress—is not unpleasing, though the dual portrait of Don Antonio Ugarte and his wife seems to us unattractive, both in colour and design.

San Sebastián.　　　　St. Sebastian.
Saint Sébastien.　　Der heilige Sebastian.

CASTIGLIONE

Diógenes.   Diogenes.
Diogène.   Diogenes.

LUIS PARET

Baile de máscaras.   Masked Ball.
Bal masqué.   Maskenball

Angel portador de la Eucaristía.   Angel Bearing the Eucharist.
Ange porteur de l'Eucharistie.   Engel Träger der Eucharistie.

VICENTE LOPEZ

La Reina Doña María Cristina de Borbón.
La Reine Marie Christine de Bourbon.

Queen Maria Cristina de Borbon.
Königin Maria Cristina von Borbon.

La creación de Adán y el pecado original.
La création d'Adam et le Péché originel.
The Creation of Adam and Original Sin.
Die Erschaffung Adams und Die Erbsünde

Retablo de S. Juan Bautista y Sta. Catalina.
Rétable de St. Jean Baptiste et Ste. Catherine.
Retablo of St. John Baptist and St. Catherine.
Altartafel von St. Johannes des Täufers und Heil. Katharina.

El martirio de Santa Inés.   The Martyrdom of St. Agnes.
Le martyre de Sainte Agnès.   Martyrium der Heiligen Agnes.

La Virgen y el Niño.   Virgin and Child.
La Vierge et l'Enfant.   Die Jungfrau und das Kind.

La Reina María de Inglaterra.   Mary Tudor of England.
La Reine Marie d'Angleterre.   Königin Maria von England.

Dama y niña.   Lady and Child.
Dame et enfant   Dame und Kind.

La Sagrada Familia «del Pajarito».
La Sainte Famille «à l'Oiselet».

The Holy Family.
Die Heilige Familie.

San Pablo ermitaño. Saint Paul the Hermit.
Saint Paul premier ermite. S. Paulus eremita.

La cena de S. Benito.　　　　St. Benedict's Supper.
La cène de Saint Benoît.　　Abendmahl des heiligen Benediktus.

Retrato de Iwanowitz.
Portrait d'Iwanowitz.

Portrait of Iwanowitz.
Bildnis von Iwanowitz.

JUAN BTA. DEL MAZO

Cacería del Tabladillo, en Aranjuez.   Hunting-party in Aranjuez.
Partie de chasse du Tabladillo à Aranjuez.   Die Jagd des Tabladillo in Aranjuez.

GROUND FLOOR

If we enter the Ground Floor of the Prado by the North door, we find ourselves in a circular vestibule where there are a number of battle scenes painted by Snayers (1592-1667?). On the left there is a small hall, artificially illuminated, containing an extremely interesting fresco brought here from the Segovian village of Maderuelo.

This unique fresco was painted by an unknown Spanish artist of the XIIth. century. It was removed from the Hermitage of Maderuelo, where it was in danger of being entirely lost and, although some fragments are lacking, it is now well preserved against further deterioration.

The two main themes displayed over the entrance door are *The Creation of Adam* and *Original Sin*, both painted with the extreme simplicity of this very early period. The Segovian fresco has greatly enriched the Prado's collection of early Spanish art, and it forms an interesting introduction to the study of succeeding centuries, of which the building contains so many splendid examples.

> After seeing the Maderuelo fresco visitors are advised to enter the hall devoted to Spanish retable paintings, which is to be found at the end of the Rotunda, where there is also specially designed artificial lighting.

HALL L

Here there is a small, but representative, collection of Spanish Gothic painting, including the earliest works in the possession of the Prado.

Impartial study reveals that although XVth. century Spanish painting is of real interest, it cannot be compared with contemporary Flemish work, which had mastered the art of oil-painting to a degree that was not achieved in Spain for another century and a half.

Two retables, each portraying three figures, and a number of fragments from others, are now before us. The first is the work of an unknown Castilian artist, and is called the *Retable of Don Sancho de Rojas* after the Archbishop who commissioned it for the Monastery of St. Benito el Real. It was bought by the Prado in 1929.

The second, dedicated to the Virgin Mary and St. Francis of Assisi, was bought one year later. It was originally found in a farmhouse near the village of La Bañeza, and is the work of Nicolás Francés who died in 1468. Both are of great beauty, though inferior to other panels to be seen here, such as *St. John the Baptist and St. Catherine* which came from the Los Arcos Chapel in Sigüenza Cathedral. This, together with four others belonging to the same group, is the work of the unknown artist called the Master of Sigüenza, at some date between 1430 and 1450, and was bought by the Prado in 1930.

In our opinion, there is no example of Spanish primitive painting to equal this panel, either for its brilliant colouring or for the serene beauty of St. Catherine.

Among the other panels on exhibition here the fine colouring of Pedro García de Benabarre's *Martyrdom of Saints Sebastian and Policarpo* should not be overlooked. Pedro García was born in the village of Benabarre early in the XVth. century. There is another retable signed by him to be seen in the Barcelona Gallery.

The two panels portraying *The Transference of the Body of St. James the Elder* came from a Church near Lérida, and formed part of the Bosch legacy. The artist is unknown, though he is believed to have belonged to the Aragonese School of the early XVth. century. Both are in a good state of preservation, and reveal the same remarkable vividness of colour.

In the opinion of one critic the author of the full-length panel *St. Vincent,* known as the Master of Archbishop Dalmau de Mur, is entitled to be named «the greatest of the Aragonese Masters of the mid-fifteenth century», and the extraordinary realism, finish and the advanced technique certainly merit the claim that he be considered «the Aragonese Jaime Huguet». *St. Vincent* came to the Prado in 1920 from the Madrid Archaeological Museum, in whose possession it had been since it reached the capital from Saragossa in 1871.

There is a small *Head of a Prophet* by Jaime Huguet which, though finely painted, is not the equal of those by the same XIVth. century Catalán painter to be seen in Barcelona.

The panels illustrating *The Story of St. Michael*, ascribed to the Master of Arguis, also came from their original village Church, reaching the Prado via the Archaeological Museum. The Master of Arguis is another early XVth. century Aragonese painter, his work being particularly notable for what has been described as its «narrative easiness».

HALL XLIX

This contains Spanish Paintings of the XVth. and XVIth. centuries.

Over a century ago the Museo de la Trinidad obtained six religious pictures by an unknown painter, known as the Master of La Sisla, from the Monastery of la Sisla, near Toledo, and these came into the possession of the Prado in 1872. The two most interesting are the *Adoration of the Magi*, and the *Death of the Virgin Mary*, believed to have been painted between 1480 and 1520.

The Prado contains three panels by Vicente Juan Masip, two circular and one oval. These are *The Visitation, The Martyrdom of St. Agnes* and *The Coronation of the Virgen Mary*, which were bought for the Prado by King Ferdinand VIIth. the circular panels for 9.000 «reales» in 1826, and the oval one, two years later, for 3.000. They were catalogued, until 1920, as being by Juan de Juanes.

The best, in our opinion, is *The Martyrdom of St. Agnes*, which closely resembles the work of Raphael, though *The Visitation* is only a shade less remarkable. The figures of St. Agnes and her

executioner are finely portrayed, without any of the over-dramatiz-
ation from which such a subject might easily suffer.

We must now draw the visitor's attention to the two versions
of *Virgin and Child,* numbered 944 and 946; the portrait of Beato
Juan de Ribera, and the *Presentation of the Infant Jesus* by Luis
de Morales.

Morales belongs to his period, which is that of the religious
panel revealing both Italian and Flemish influences. Although his
modelling is occasionally effeminate his best works show both a
sincere religious feeling and a subtle perception of human emotion,
which entitle him to be considered the best Spanish painter of the
XVth. century, with the exception of El Greco.

His *Virgin and Child,* which formed part of the Bosch legacy
(numbered 2.655; see Hall LXVIII), is generally considered the
best work of its kind by Morales. A critic wrote on this subject,
«Apart from its own extraordinary artistic merit this masterpiece is
of particular interest as revealing the profound influence of the
Renaissance upon Morales. The harmonious design and the finely
drawn hands, so obviously copied from life, show that, although
himself a disciple of a northern Master, Morales was profoundly
influenced by Raphael or Michael Angelo, whom he sought to
imitate».

The Beato Ribera portrait, for, which it is believed that the
venerable Juan de Villegas served as model, was presented to the
Prado in 1896 by Doña María Enríquez de Valdés. The pale face,
vibrant with personality, is beautifully executed. *The Presentation
of the Infant Jesus,* bought by King Charles IVth., is also vivid
with colour and movement, the best figure being that of the young
girl passing before the Child and carrying a lighted candle. On
the other hand, the figure of Jesus appears out of proportion,
and the grouping is over-crowded.

A very interesting picture in this gallery is also that
known as *The Virgin of the Knight of Montesa* so named because
of the portrait of the Knight beside the figure of St. Bernard. It
was purchased by the Prado for 100.000 pesetas from Lorenzo Al-
barrán in 1920. It belongs to the Valencian School of Rodrigo de
Osona, and was painted in the last years of the XVth. century.

The colouring is vivid, and the heads of both the Virgin and St. Benito are finely portrayed.

Juan Correa de Vivar was a little known Castilian painter of the XVIth. century. Although not a great master he was one of the best exponents of the Italian style that was so strongly influencing Spanish art at that period. His work resembles that of Juan de Juanes, though it also contains certain similarities with his contemporary Morales.

Of the eight pictures by Correa in the Prado the finest is undoubtedly his *Death of the Virgin Mary*. Painted for the Church of El Tránsito in Toledo it came here from the Museo de la Trinidad in 1872. It possesses an effective sense of restraint, combined with excellent design.

Hernando Yáñez de la Almedina is one of the XVIth. century Spanish painters who most faithfully reflects the lessons of the Italian Renaissance. Although a disciple of Leonardo da Vinci, and with his Master's exquisite presentation of detail, his work has a distinctive quality of its own, which is immediately obvious in his splendid panel *St. Catherine*, once the property of the Marqués de Casa Argudín, and which reached the Prado in 1946. The vivid red of the Saint's robe, and the masterly design of the figure as a whole, mark it as a work of the highest order.

There is another vigorous half-length painting by Yáñez entitled *St. Damian*, concerning which we shall have more to say later.

Pedro Machuca was not only a painter, but also a sculptor and architect, and the only example of his work in the possession of the Prado is his *Virgin Mary Comforting the Souls in Purgatory*, which was painted in Italy in 1517, and came to Spain direct from Spoleto in 1935. Don Manuel Gómez Moreno, who made a special study of Machuca, says: «Machuca is clearly not a genius, but he does not lack originality, and devoted great pains in his employment of colour. The tones of the panel are cold, but the work is finely finished.»

The Descent from the Cross is magnificent picture.

Juan de Juanes was known as «the Spanish Raphael», but his picture, *The Last Supper*, possesses little outstanding merit. His reputation, which once stood very high, has fallen in recent times, though a male portrait by him in the same gallery gives a better idea of his capabilities. Although not remarkable, *The Last Supper* will bear comparison with contemporary works by the Flemish and Italian Masters. It is believed to be part of the series of five panels, which are on exhibition on the Ground Floor of the Prado, painted by Juan de Juanes for the Valencian Church of St. Esteban, later bought by King Charles IVth. *The Last Supper* was looted by the French during the Napoleonic invasion, but was returned to Spain in 1818, being valued at 250.000 «reales» in 1834. At that period it was regarded as a masterpiece, but today is recognized as little more than a copy of the world-famous da Vinci fresco, though Juanes' St. John—his face alight with love as he gazes at Jesus—is a fine and moving piece of original work.

The portrait of Don Luis de Castellá (for many years believed to be of Don Luis de Castelvi) was also bought in Valencia by King Charles IVth, and appears in the catalogue of the Royal Collection in 1814. It is an interesting study, and suggests that Juan de Juanes might have been better advised if he had devoted himself to portrait painting instead of to the conventional religious themes of the period.

We now come to the first Spanish painter who was prepared to make portraiture his main interest—Alonso Sánchez Coello— disciple of the outstanding Dutch portrait painter, Antonio Moro, who paid three visits to Spain at the invitation of King Philip IInd. There are portraits of no less than four Kings by Coello on exhibition in the Prado. His work is accurate and careful and, although he never attempted to achieve Greco's uncanny penetration into the minds of his models, he is revealed as an acute observer with a fine sense of colour.

Madrazo said of Coello, «his work contains many of the best elements of the Flemish and Venetian Schools and, although he can never rival Titian, Raphael or Holbein, his portraits are well executed, and he makes use of a distinctive, though pleasing, range of cold tones to achieve his effects».

Coello's portrait of King Philip IInd. in mourning is particularly interesting and reveals the pale, fanatic face, compressed lips and keen, cold gaze—so strangely lacking in all sense of human kindness—that stamped this monarch's personality so strongly upon his times. It was looted by the French during the Napoleonic invasion, but returned to Spain in 1816, entering the Prado 11 years later. For many years it was attributed to Coello's pupil Pantoja. The canvases of the ill-fated Prince Charles and Isabel Clara, painted in 1558 and 1579 respectively, are distinguished examples of Spanish portraiture before the genius of Velázquez had created new world standards.

The Betrothal of St. Catherine, signed and dated 1578, additionally reveals a deplorable confusion between St. Catherine of Siena and St. Catherine of Alexandria. It was sold by the artist for 150 ducats, and was in the Escorial until 1839.

Coello's famous disciple, Juan Pantoja de la Cruz, never quite achieved his Master's eminence, but there are two vigorous canvases by him, *St. Augustin* and *St. Nicholas de Tolentino,* which reveal him to be an equal as a painter, even though lacking Coello's mastery of design and form.

Both are signed and dated 1601. Originally in the Colegio de Doña María de Aragón, they came to the Prado in 1933, from the Museo de la Trinidad.

HALLS LIII, LIII A AND LIV

In Halls LIII and LIII A are temporarily exhibited a great number of Goya' drawings of the collection owned by the Museum.

The Hall LIV contains some of Goya's less successful works, such as his *Crucifixion* and *Holy Family*.

The group portrait of the Osuna family reveals not only the brilliance, but also the occasional carelessness to which Goya confesses in his writings, a carelessness which is particularly evident in his commissioned work, as opposed to his paintings of a subject of his own selection.

HALLS LV, LVI AND LVII

These three halls were decorated in 1928, in the style of a XVIIIth. century palace, for the exhibition of Goya's «cartoons», or pictures for tapestries, and contain furniture appropriate to the period. The canvases, in their attractive gilded frames, are not hung, but are placed leaning against the walls. Their total of forty-one includes nearly all the designs ever made by Goya for the Royal Tapestry Works of Santa Bárbara.

In a book by Cruzada Villaamil, published in 1870, on the subject of these pictures, the author lists 45, from which 92 tapestries, worth 600.000 «reales», were woven, Goya himself receiving 189.000 «reales» for the work.

The present Prado catalogue also lists a total of 45, though only 38 of these were mentioned by Cruzada Villaamil, the other seven having been discovered or identified since 1870. Among these latter are the first and last of a not particularly interesting series of eleven, begun by Goya before the year 1776 and terminated in 1791, which are entitled, respectively, *Picnic on the Banks of the River Manzanares* and *Blind man's Buff*. Goya was just 30 when Mengs recommended him for the post as one of the artists who designed the tapestries for the Royal Factory, which had been established half a century earlier. He began work there in 1776 and, to begin with, his pictures are few and of no outstanding merit. However, the opportunity afforded him invaluable experience in the composition of canvases that ultimately captured, as no other artist has ever done, the dances, picnics, plays and bull-fights that together went to make up life in Madrid during the last quarter of the XVIIIth. century. As such they represent not only a welcome break with the old style preoccupation for mythological, religious or historic themes, but also afford us an invaluable and vivid glimpse of the period.

Goya's tapestries were made to decorate Royal Palaces, but his pictures reveal that his absorbing interest was in the common people. He was passionately attached to his work, and contrived to leave the mark of his special genius upon every one of his pictures. He delivered no less than 24 of the total of 45 exhibited here during the years 1777, 1778 and 1779: four belong to the year 1786, another four to 1787, two to 1788 and three to 1791. All are oil-paintings upon a red-tinted linen cloth, which has tended to darken with the passage of time more than might have been wished.

Some of these «cartoons» are the earliest of Goya's works in the possession of the Prado.

For his *Picnic on the Banks of the Manzanares* he was paid 7.000 «reales» and, for *The Dance*, 8.000. For *The Quarrel*, *The Maja and the Hooded Man*, *The Wine Bibbers*, and *The Parasol*, all delivered to the Tapestry Works during the course of the year 1777, he received a total of 17.000 «reales». *The Picnic* is not the equal of either *The Dance* or *The Maja and the Hooded Man*, and the three painted during 1778—*The Blind Guitar Player*, *The Fiesta of Madrid* and *The Crockery Seller*—are particularly fine. Among Goya's work completed during 1786 mention must be made of *The Vintage*—in our opinion the best of the series—*The Flower Sellers*, and *The Injured Builder*. In the same vein are *The Snowfall*, and *The Wedding*, both painted in 1787, and *Las Gigantillas* and *Los Zancos* belonging to the following years. Finally, in 1791, came *The Nincompoop* and *Blind Man's Buff*. Though many people are of the opinion that Goya's greatest work is not to be found among these «cartoons» for tapestry, it is unquestionable that they are more typical of him than any others, with their graceful portrayal of the clothes and customs of the people, and the rich colouring of which the artist was always master. Although Goya enjoyed making these pictures they were the source of many complaints from the tapestry workers, who claimed that the number of figures, and their vari-coloured clothes, presented inmense technical difficulties for the weavers, and that the artist's paintings were too detailed, and his models too complex, to lend themselves readily to reproduction.

Cruzada Villaamil wrote of them, «Goya must have had both pleasant and unpleasant memories of his work for the Tapestry Works. The pleasant aspect lay in the fact that these pictures were responsible for drawing the attention of the Court to his work, and so led directly to his successful career as official Court Painter; the unpleasant associations being provoked by the spectacle of his original models being indifferently reproduced in another medium, many people judging his capacity by the reproductions rather than from the original paintings».

It is a fact that they were considered so unimportant for many years after Goya's death that they laid almost forgotten in one of the cellars of the Royal Palace until 1869 when, after careful restoration, they appeared in the Prado catalogue of the year 1876.

HALL LVII A

From Hall LVII we pass on to Hall LVII A, where there are on exhibition several paintings by Goya; two portraits, of Carlos IVth. and Queen María Luisa, two still-life studies, several «cartoons» for tapestry and the most beautiful piece in the Hall, entitled: *La Pradera de San Isidro.*

The small *Pradera de San Isidro* was also bought from the Osuna collection in 1896, the price paid for this delightful example of Goya's art being 15.000 pesetas.

HALL LVI A

Here you may see the macabre paintings with which Goya decorated the walls of his home between the years 1819 and 1823, when the lonely and deaf old man was nearing the end of his long life. They are oil-paintings, having been saved for posterity by Baron Emil d'Erlanger who, in 1873, bought Goya's old house and employed the expert, Don Salvador Martínez Cubells, to transpose these wall-drawings to canvas. It seems likely that if Baron d'Erlanger had not done this the paintings would have been totally destroyed by the action of time and neglect.

After exhibiting them in the 1878 Paris Universal Exhibition they were presented to the Spanish Government in 1881, and appeared in the Prado the following year.

The black fantasies that dominated this period of Goya's life do not appeal to the general public, though modern critics regard these sinister glimpses into a haunted mind as masterly, and have described them as the «culmination of the demoniac aspect of Goya's genius». It is difficult to realise that the hand that scored the harsh outlines to the «black paintings» was the same as that which wrought the silver tones in the portrait of Bayeu, and the repulsive figures in the «Witches' Sabbath» seem unimaginable from the artist responsible for the serene harmony of the portraits of Silvela or of Doña Tadea Arias.

HALL LV A

The Moncloa Executions is a picture of terrifying vividness. In our opinion this and *The Lances* are the two finest historical canvases in the Prado but, although they can thus be compared with each other, they clearly emphasize the essential difference between the two great artists. This lies in the fact that whereas Velázquez was content to record history, Goya was a propagandist, passionately concerned to convert the beholder to his own opinion as to the rights and wrongs of the events he records. Velázquez, with the detachment of an historian, confines himself to depicting the episode; Goya, on the other hand, violently expresses his personal sympathy for the ragged and desperate people of Spain in their seemingly hopeless struggle against the remorseless perfection of Napoleon's military machine. Something of the artist's own hatred for the invaders has inspired his painting of the huddled group of Spaniards, with their stark gestures of despair exposed in a nightmare glare of light. To Goya the French executioners were devoid of all humanity, simply a line of faceless uniformed figures, their heads crouched over the sights of their rifles, and it is in the dramatic contrast between this inhuman line of executioners and the passionate despair of their victims, that the picture's greatness lies.

The canvas shows unmistakable signs of having been painted at top speed, and in the white-heat of the artist's own intense emotion. Its companion piece, depicting the attack by the Spanish crowd upon some of Napoleon's coloured troops in the Puerta del Sol, although fine, is less effective than *The Executions*, owing to its confused design.

It is believed that Goya painted both these pictures in 1814, when he was specially commissioned, for 1.500 «reales», to perpetuate the heroic deeds of the rebellion against Napoleon. Both came to the Prado, valued at 8.000 «reales», in 1834, and were listed in the catalogue of 1872.

Goya painted from the heart, and he obviously disliked doing the conventional Court portraits that were occasionally required of him. Both the portraits of King Ferdinand VIIth—and the same may be said of that of General Palafox—are almost caricatures. The personal contempt for the King which Goya undoubtedly felt, is barely concealed, though his natural genius now and then dominates his feelings, as can be seen in his drawing of the head of Palafox, and again in the fine colouring employed in the figure of Ferdinand.

Goya's signed head and shoulders self-portraits in oils also came to the Prado via the Museo de la Trinidad from its original owner, Don Román de la Huerta. There is a duplicate which, in our opinion, is the better of the two, to be seen in the Academia de San Fernando, dated 1815.

On exhibit in this Hall are two paintings dating from Goya's last days: the portrait of Muguiro, signed «Don Juan de Muguiro by his friend Goya, at 81 years of age in Bordeaux, May 1827», and the painting, also signed, entitled *The Milkmaid of Bordeaux*, in which the great master's fluid, vibrant brushwork, and the freshness of colour anticipate by many years the birth of the «impressionist» school.

In order to preserve the essential sequence in time it is now necessary to cross the vestibule, numbered XLVII, and enter that devoted to sculptury, which is situated immediately below Velázquez's hall. On the right there is a door leading to 13 halls. numbered LIX to LXIII ₐ.

HALL LIX

This is devoted to Flemish and German artists of the first half of the XVIth. century.

The outstanding Flemish painter of the period was Ambrosious Benson, represented by seven panels illustrating religious themes. The German Christopher Amberger has two portraits on exhibition, believed to be of the goldsmith Jörg Zörer and his wife, which reveal the characteristics of the «primitive» German school. Both portraits were catalogued in La Granja Palace in 1746.

Benson's panels originally formed part of the retable of Santa Cruz in Segovia, and reached the Prado from the Museo de la Trinidad.

The collection, as a whole, does not compare with the best Flemish work of the XVth. century.

Pieter Coecke Van Aelst's triptych, *The Adoration of the Magi*, is in no way outstanding and, in our opinion, the head and shoulders entitled *The Saviour*, ascribed to Jan Massys, or Metsys—son of the more famous Quentin Metsys—is far superior, as are also Van Oostsanen's *St. Jerome*, the *St. Francis* by one Van Orley's disciples, and the *Figure of Zachary* by Jan Prevost.

HALL LX

Here there are 15 portraits by Anthony Moor; the remarkable, *The Money Changer and his Wife*, by Marinus Claeszon van Reymerswaele—a legacy from the Duke of Tarifa in 1934—and the really beautiful *Portrait of a Humanist* by Jan van Scorel, bought by the Prado in the following year.

The Money Changer and his Wife, signed and dated 1539, is a brilliant character study, showing the acute concentration upon both faces, while their hands are counting the money before them.

The Dutchman Moor—known in this country as Moro—is considered the founder of Spanish portrait painting, and here we may study some of his best works. Outstanding are four portraits of women, the artist's wife Metgen, painted in 1554; that of Mary Tudor of England, wife and aunt of King Philip IInd. of Spain; thirdly, that of the wife of the Emperor Maximilian IInd., María of Austria, dated 1551 and, lastly, of Mary Tudor's intimate friend the Duchess of Feria, which belongs to a later period.

Additionally, there are full-length studies of the Emperor Maximilian IInd, and of the Court Jester Pejeron, both of which fully display Anthony Moor's remarkable genius.

The fact that he is more interested in the drawing, than in the colouring of his pictures reveals Moor's northern origin. He does not attempt the minuteness of detail typical of his great contemporary Holbein (the Younger), but his work is both vigorous and penetrating.

Some critics have failed to give Moor his just share of praise, Reinach not even mentioning him in his *Apollo*, but it is now generally admitted that no history of portrait painting in Europe is complete without some reference to him.

Probably the best single example of Moor's art is his portrait of his wife Metgen, with a richer colouring and lighter finish than is usual with him. A close second choice would be that of Mary Tudor, painted in the year of her marriage with King Philip, eleven years her junior. The Emperor Charles Vth. liked it so much that, when he retired to die in the Monastery of Yuste, he took it with him.

HALL LX A

The Flemish painters Michel Coxcie, Jan Sanders van Hemesen and Otto van Veen and the Dutch Marinus Claeszon van Reymerswaele, Adriaen Cronenburch and Jan van Scorel share this Hall. Among the paintings hung hére the following are worthy of mention: the several portraits of ladies and children signed by Cronenburch, painted in a rather severe but nevertheless firm and detailed style; the *Virgin with Child* and *St. Jerome* by Van Reymerswaele, characteristic of the «contorsioned» style of this great painter; the painting by Van Scorel entitled *The Universal Flood*, an interesting work with powerful composition and, finally, the great triptyche by Coxcie on the life of the Virgin, painted for a church in Brussels and acquired by King Philip IInd. The centre panel of this triptyche, showing «The death of the Virgin» is contains a number of interesting figures and the colouring is sumptuous.

HALLS LXI, LXI A, LXII AND LXII A

Halls LXI and LXII are dedicated to Murillo; the other two (LXI A and LXII A), to Ribera. In Hall LXII we find also paintings by Valdés Leal, Juan de Sevilla, Alonso Miguel de Tovar and the Basque landscape painter Ignacio Iriarte, and in Hall LXII A, Zurbarán and Ribalta.

This Halls is dominated by Murillo and Ribera, whose styles have often been described, respectively, as «soft» and «rough», though the superficiality of this analysis becomes obvious as soon as we examine the examples of both artists to be seen here. Immediately a certain similarity between the supposed oppossite extremes begins to emerge, particularly hen we observe the essentially Spanish quality of both, even though Ribera was working in Naples and Murillo in Seville.

Both Murillo and Ribera were intensely realistic in their style, a fact which is clearly revealed in their religious painting, where their figures of saints are untouched by the conventional idealization to be found in all the non-Spanish artists of the XVIth. and XVIIth. centuries.

This hall contains the following works by Murillo; *The Holy Family «del Pajarito», The Adoration of the Shepherds, The Annunciation, St. Anne and the Child Virgin,* a half-length *Conception, The Vision of St. Francis, Rebecca and Eleazar, St. Augustin between Christ and the Virgin, The Martyrdom of St. Andrew,* and various other smaller pictures.

In the presence of this further collection of Murillo and Ribera —with whose paintings we are already familiar from the First Floor— the vigorous and earthy quality of the latter, and the mellow finish so typical of the former, become still further apparent.

Perhaps the most famous of Murillo's works on exhibition here is his *Holy Family,* showing the Virgin Mary, St. Joseph and the Infant Jesus. The Infant is shown playing with a small white dog, and the whole composition is of rare tenderness and charm. It was painted in 1650 and, nearly a century later, was mentioned in the catalogue of the Palace of La Granja as forming part of Elizabeth Farnesio's collection. Napoleon's brother Joseph carried it off to France, from whence it was returned in 1818. In 1794 it was valued at 12.000 «reales».

Another of Murillo's canvases looted during the French invasion was *The Adoration of the Shepherds.* This was painted at the same period as Velázquez's *Maids of Honour* and *The Spinners,* and was valued at 30.000 «reales» in 1794. It provides an excellent example of the realistic treatment of religious themes that was so marked a characteristic of Spanish XVIIth. century art. This is also true of the tranquil «interior» portraying St. Anne teaching her little daughter the Virgin Mary, a picture which was valued at 6.000 «reales» in 1794, and which also once formed part of the Elizabeth Farnesio's collection.

The Vision of St. Francis and *St. Augustin between Christ and the Virgin Mary* form a pair for an altar-piece.

The former was bought by King Charles IVth, and the latter by the Marqués de los Llanos.

There are four small oil-paintings by Murillo on exhibition here, which served as preliminary sketches for the finished canvases in the possession of the London collector Otto Beit, on the theme of the Prodigal Son. These sketches were in the Royal Palace in Madrid in 1814, and appear in the first Prado catalogue. It is believed that they were painted towards the end of Murillo's life.

With the *Murillos* to be seen here, together with those already visited on the First Floor, it is possible to form a clear impression of the artist's work as a whole. His style is gentle and uncomplex and, in its intimate simplicity, is perhaps better suited to the home than to the decoration of Church or Palace. He was far more attracted to the portrayal of gentle Virgins and smiling Infant Christs than he was to the dramatic and terrible scenes of Christ's Passion and Death.

Despite changing fashions in Art, Murillo will never lack for admirers. Gerardo Diego recognized that the Spanish people—and women especially—have never wavered in their loyalty to Murillo, whatever may be the fluctuations of his prestige in other countries. This loyalty outweighs the carping of critics, who are often more concerned with being in the fashion of the moment than they are with the eternal verities of Art.

The Presentation of the Virgin in the Temple by Valdés Leal, and the *Rich Man's Feast and Lazarus* by Juan de Sevilla are of no outstanding interest. Sevilla was an Andalusian disciple of Pedro de Moya, who sought to follow the style of Van Dyck. Sevilla himself was a great admirer of Rubens, and his paintings clearly reveal the fact.

Pictures by Zurbarán. The signed, *St. Jacob de la Marca*, originally painted for the Chapel of St. Diego in Alcalá de Henares, was in the Museo de la Trinidad before it reached the Prado and, in 1933, was on exhibition in the Madrid Church of San Francisco el Grande.

St. Lucas Contemplating the Crucifix, brought to the Prado

La resurrección de la carne.
La résurrection de la chair.

The Resurrection of the Flesh.
Die Wiederauferstehung des Fleisches

DAVID TENIERS

Fiesta campestre.   A Country Fair.

BRUEGHEL DE VELOURS

La vista.
La vue.

Sight.
Gesicht

El Bautismo de Cristo.   The Baptism of Christ.
Le Baptême de Christ.   Die Taufe Christi.

PANTOJA

La Reina Margarita de Austria. The Queen Margaret of Austria.
La Reine Marguerite d'Autriche. Königin Margarete von Oesterreich.

El baile de S. Antonio de la Florida.
La danse de S. Antonio de la Florida.

The Dance of S. Antonio de la Florida.
Der Tanz von S. Antonio de la Florida.

La cometa.

GOYA

Aquelarre (fragmento).
Sabbat (détail).

Witches'Sabbath (detail).
Aquelarre (fragment).

GOYA

Los fusilamientos de la Moncloa.　　The Moncloa Executions
Les fusillements de la Moncloa.　　Erschiessungen bei der Moncloa.

María Luisa de Borbón.

Gran Duquesa de Toscaña.	Great Duchess of Toscana.
Grande Duchesse de Toscane.	Grossherzogin von Toscana.

Retrato de un eclesiástico.
Portrait d'un ecclésiastique.

Portrait of a Clergyman.
Bildnis eines Geistlichen.

LUCCA GIORDANO

La muerte del centauro Neso.   The Death of the Centaur Neso.
La morte du centaure Neso.   Der Tod des Zentauren Nessus.

Por traer cañutos
de diablos de Bayona

Dibujo.   Drawing.
Dessin.   Zeichnungen.

Grupo llamado «de San Ildefonso».
(¿Cástor y Polux?)

La Dama de Elche.

Joyas del «Tesoro del Delfín».
Joyaux du «Trésor du Dauphin».

Jewels of the «Dauphin's Treasure».
Schmuckstücken von «Schatz des Dauphin».

in 1936, is interesting because of the theory that the figure of St. Lucas may have been a self-portrait of Zurbarán.

The still-life picture, catalogued as No. 2803, was a gift from the politician Don Francisco Cambó. It is ascribed to Zurbarán, though there are some doubts on the point. In any case it is a very fine example of that artist's style in treating a non-religious subject.

Ribera painted with a much more virile brush, specializing in rough, bearded types, that would never have interested Murillo.

Nevertheless, Ribera's *Trinity* contains some charming figures of young angels, which shows that he was not insensitive to conventional physical beauty, but was more interested in the portrayal of character than his younger contemporary.

Special mention must be made of Ribera's oil-painting entitled, *The Duelling Women,* signed and dated 1636, which is said to record an incident which had taken place in Naples 84 years previously in the presence of the Marqués del Vasto. Two women, whose names are not known, fought a duel to decide which of them should take the man whom they both sought for her lover. History records that blood was shed, but does not tell us whether either of the duellists was killed by her rival.

The *Conception* to be seen here is inferior to Ribera's famous one in Salamanca—known as *La Concepción de Monterrey*—and is also not so fine as Murillo's rendering of the same theme. It was bought for 12.000 «reales» by King Ferdinand VIIth. in 1833.

The subject of the Immaculate Conception was particularly popular with baroque artists, and the best Spanish examples are undoubtedly those by Murillo and Ribera.

The half-length *St. Sebastian* is notable for Ribera's brilliant modelling of the saint's body. It belongs to the Master's last years, and once hung in Velázquez's studio, later becoming the property of Queen María Luisa's favourite Godoy. Ribera painted the *Martyrdom of St. Sebastián* several times, and those on exhibition in the Bilbao and Valencia Galleries are both superior to that possessed by the Prado.

It is believed that Ribera's *Fable of Bacchus* was one of his finest works, but it was destroyed in the great fire that burned down the old Royal Palace in 1734, and we have before us only two fragments that were somehow saved. They are of two ivy-crowned profiles—one a woman and the other of an old man—and reveal entirely new aspects of Ribera's art. They are catalogued 1122 and 1123.

St. Paul the Hermit (numbered 1075 in the Catalogue), signed and dated 1640; and the second the portrait of the blind sculptor Giovanni Gambassi, also signed and dated 1632. Both bear the unmistakable characteristics of the artist who has been described as «the leader of XVIIth. century Spanish painting».

Examples of the work of Ribera are to be seen here, as well as later in Halls LXI A and LXII A.

HALL LXIII

Paintings by Alonso Cano and Carreño.

Alonso Cano, painter, sculptor and architect, influenced Spanish XVIIth. century art in much the same way as Michael Angelo inspired that of Italy during the preceding century. The Prado contains nine pictures by him.

Among those before us now are the following four outstanding canvases; two versions of *Christ Supported by an Angel*, *The Virgin and Child*, and *St. Benedict's Vision*. *St. Benedict's Vision* is listed in the catalogue of the Alcázar Palace in Madrid for the year 1700, while the *Virgin and Child* was bought by King Charles IVth. Of the two versions of *Christ Supported by an Angel*, one was bought from the Marqués de la Ensenada in 1769, and the other—the only signed one—came to the Prado under the Bosch legacy.

There is no recorded work by Alonso Cano which entitles him to be considered a really great artist, despite the rich colouring of his paintings in Granada Cathedral, and various of his canvases here in the Prado which are also deserving of admiration.

Cano began his apprenticeship in Seville at the same time as Velázquez and Zurbarán but, unlike his great contemporaries, Cano was less sure of the line he wished to pursue and, like Michael Angelo, was really more interested in sculpture than in painting. However, his pictures are nearly always of a very high quality, and some, such as his *St. Agnes* now in the Berlin Museum.

have all the characteristics to be found in the best of Zurbarán's works. The silver and grey tones employed by Cano bring some of Velázquez's portraits to mind but, occasionally, his colouring is harsh and unclear. In short, Alonso Cano was a painter of uneven quality, though always displaying a sense of taste and beauty in the mature and classic style of the XVIIth. century.

The painter with largest number of works on exhibition in this hall is Juan Carreño (1614-1685). These consist of two on religious themes—*St. Anne Instructing the Virgin* and *St. Sebastian*—and three full-length portraits, of Peter Ivanovitch Potemkin, of Francisco Bazán, a Court Jester; and the deformed child Eugenia Martínez Vallejo, one of them a nude study.

The four portraits were already in the Royal collection at the end of the XVIIth. century. King Ferdinand VIIth. presented the nude to the painter Juan Gálvez and, after passing through various hands, it reached the Prado in 1939 from Baron de Forna. The clothed study of the same unattractive subject came to the Prado in 1828, when it was attributed to Velázquez, though with the rider «ascribed by some people to Carreño».

Don Juan Carreño de Miranda was of a noble Asturian family, and is considered one of the most eminent of Spanish portraitists, even being compared to Velázquez though, in our opinion, without justification. The Prado contains seven portraits by Carreño, those of King Charles IInd. and his mother Queen Mariana, being in the Central Gallery, while that of the Duke of Pastrana is in the hall principally devoted to Velázquez, of which we have already had something to say.

This is enough to enable us to judge of his quality, and to appreciate his sense of realism and technical excellence in the Velázquez tradition. Cean Bermúdez wrote that Carreño was «the finest naturalist painter in the Castile of his day», though, in our opinion, Cossío was nearer the truth when he described him as «the greatest of all the Madrid School, with the sole exception of Velázquez».

While the nude study of the deformed child cannot be made attractive, Carreño manages to prevent it from being repulsive, and the modelling of the body is beautifully executed.

HALL LXIII A

Pictures by Antonio del Castillo, Esteban March, Friar Juan Rizi, Herrera «el Viejo» and Antonio Puga.

Friar Juan Rizi's *St. Benedict's Supper* is a most powerful and moving portrayal of a scene illuminated by artificial light, in which the sober, yet intense colouring makes a strong appeal to the senses.

It was painted for the Monastery of St. Millan de la Cogolla, and reached the Prado from the Museo de la Trinidad.

Among the series of six canvases, illustrating the Old Testament story of Joseph by the Cordoban painter Antonio del Castillo, two are the most notable. These are entitled, *Joseph Sold into Captivity* and *The Chastity of Joseph*.

They were intended for the Museo de la Trinidad, but came to the Prado in 1863, when they were purchased for 9.000 pesetas.

Neither is of outstanding merit, Castillo's style, in the opinion of Madrazo, being comparable to that of Caravaggio, and «distinguished by its harsh blending of co our».

HALL LXIV

The Hall LXIV exhibits paintings by Mateo Cerezo, Jusepe Leonardo, Francisco Rizi, Pereda, Juan Bautista del Mazo, Carreño and Claudio Coello.

Claudio Coello's *The Infant Christ* was bought by the Prado in 1935 from a Madrid antiquary. For many years it was in France, where it was ascribed to Carlo Dolci. However, when it was cleaned Coello's signature was discovered, together with the date 1660, when the artist must have been only 18 years old.

There are very few works by the XVIIth. century Aragonese artist Jusepe Leonardo, whose career was cut short by insanity before he was 40. The Prado contains three of his canvases, two of them on historical themes which may be seen on the 1st. Floo-

and the religious picture, now before us, entitled *The Birth of the Virgin Mary*. The first two were ordered by King Philip IVth. for the Salon de Reinos in the Retiro Palace, while the *Birth of the Virgin* was bought for the Museo de la Trinidad in 1864 for 10.000 «reales».

These three canvases are enough to convince us of the artist's real quality, after the Velázquez manner, and in the opinion of Señor Tormo, «if he had lived longer, and retained his faculties, he might well have become a worthy successor to Spain's greatest master».

Velázquez's inspiration is more obvious in Mazo's *Hunting Party in Aranjuez*, where the artist's special talent for landscape provides the background for various groups of figures.

It is a picture, dexterously painted in varying tones of grey, which gives us an interesting glimpse of the fashions and customs of the period. It was bought by the Prado in 1934 from a Munich collector, with funds left by the Count of Cartagena. It formed part of the Royal Collection in 1666, and was temporarily looted by Napoleon's elder brother Joseph.

Francisco Rizi (1608-1685) was the less well-known brother of Friar Juan, and the master of both José Antolínez and Claudio Coello. His *Portrait of an Artillery General* is inferior to Friar Juan's portrait of Don Tiburcio de Redin, but it possesses interest as a character study.

The portrait of a child of about 12, by an unknown artist, which may be seen here is worthy of brief special mention. It is known that the child was the son of Francisco Ramos del Manzano, a lawyer who died towards the close of the XVIIth. century. It is a sober, clear painting, in which various shades of grey are predominant, and it reveals traces of the brush of Velázquez. It was bought for the Prado for 30.000 pesetas from the antiquary Borondo in 1930.

HALL LXV

Here are a number of pictures by Ribalta, Tristán, Claudio Coello, Collantes, Orrente, Espinosa, Van der Hamen, etc.

There are four paintings by the Castilian artist Luis Tristán in the possession of the Prado, two of which are not at present on exhibition, and the other two—both of them head and shoulder representations of Saints—are before us now. In the opinion of Palomino, Tristan's work closely resembled that of Velázquez. The two examples here were both part of a retable from the Church of Yepes—a village near Toledo—and both are signed and dated 1616. They came to the Prado in 1942.

In the opinion of some experts Tristan was the real founder of the Toledo School, of which Cruzada Villaamil wrote, «it is remarkable for its pleasant and delicate use of colour which, in its purity of tone, frequently recalls the work of Titian».

It is believed that Tristan may have studied under Greco but, although some of his works were attributed to the Cretan Master, the resemblance between the two is superficial.

According to Burger, Tristan was undoubtedly influenced by Greco and, unlike so many of his contemporaries, was able to benefit by the teachings of the Venetian School without falling into the grave errors at that time being taught in Rome and Bologna.

The two heads by Tristan exhibited here are listed in the Prado catalogue as *St. Monica* and *The Weeping Saint*. Both are in a perfect state of preservation, and constitute an excellent example of Spanish painting of the late XVIth. century.

St. Matthew and St. John, is by Ribera's master, Francisco Ribalta, and has been in the possession of the Prado since the publication of its first catalogue. Commenting upon this picture, Ribalta's biographer, Espresati remarks, «the figures are depicted with a vigorous realism, and it will be observed that the hands and feet of both saints have been painted with the most minute care. The clothes are suggested, in the manner typical of Ribera towards the end of his life, by sweeping folds and heavy masses of colour».

The Prado contains only a single example of the work of the Madrid painter Francisco Collantes, who was born in the same year as Velázquez. This is *The Resurrection of the Flesh* as seen by Ezekiel, signed and dated 1630, and belonging to the Royal collection since the time of King Philip IVth. It was one of the 50 pictures sent to France at the orders of Joseph Bonaparte, but was returned in 1816. After 11 years in the Academia de San Fernando it was presented to the Prado. Palomino refers to it as «a work of great imagination and ability», while a later critic wrote, «it is a brilliant exposition of the artist's capacity as designer, colourist and anatomist, as well as a man deeply versed in architectural composition».

HALL LXVI

This is chiefly devoted to David Teniers (1610-1690) famous for his lively crowd scenes. Among the best are his *Temptation of St. Anthony, The Surgical Operation, Country Dance, The Kitchen, Pipe Smokers and Drunkards, The Alchemist, The Graceful Kitchenmaid, Country Fair, The Gay Old Man, The Pipe Smokers, The Feast of the Villagers,* and *Le Roi Boit.* All of these, though small in size, possess a golden warmth, and show us simple folk making merry in XVIIth. century Flanders.

David Teniers broke away from the tradition of painting little besides altar-pieces and religious themes, and devoted his whole energies to portraying the rich and placid life that surrounded him. Though not considered a really great artist, there is no doubt that his work portraying the customs of simple people will live because of its sincere originality.

This gallery also contains Teniers' documental, rather than artistic, portrait *The Archduke Leopold William in his Picture Gallery in Brussels,* which is signed and dated 1647. It belonged to the collection of King Philip IVth.

HALL LXVII

Jan Brueghel de Velours, born 9 years before Rubens, is the dominant artist in this room. His theme is an allegorical study of the human senses, two large canvases illustrating sight and scent, and five smaller ones of all the five physical senses. These form a series presented to King Philip IVth's younger brother, the Cardinal—Prince Don Fernando—in 1634 by the Duke of Pfalz-Neoburg. The Cardinal sold them to the Duke of Medina de las Torres who, in turn, presented them to the King in 1636.

To our taste the *Five Human Senses* appear cold and hopelessly overburdened with detail, but his studies of flowers and also some small landscape, together with his canvas *The Country Wedding*, are all exquisite of their kind.

Hall LXVII leads into a corridor bearing the number LXVIII, but its contents are of less interest. The visitor may descend a few stairs to Hall LXIX, but here, too, the Flemish pictures, and collection of sculpture and tapestry are unworthy of prolonged examination.

The alternative corridor, numbered LXX, contains a large canvas by an unknown Flemish painter of the XVIIth. century, entitled «The Beheading of St. John the Baptist», and also the «Naumaquia Romana» by Lanfranco and a «Holy Family» by Vicencio Carducho.

The visitor is advised to pass on to Hall LXXII, where there are seven portraits of the Spanish branch of the Royal House of Austria by Sánchez Coello, Pantoja and Villandrando. Here also are fifteen studies of flowers by Arellano and Bartolomé Pérez; statues of the Emperor Charles Vth. and the Empress Elizabeth; four reliefs and, inside a show-case, the collection of medals and ancient coins bequeathed to the Prado under the Bosch legacy.

The small Halls LXXI and LXXII contain, respectively, some interesting sculptury, including the famous pre-Roman «Lady of Elche», and, in five show-cases, the collection known as «The Dauphin's Treasure», of which we shall later have something to say.

From Hall LXXII the visitor passes the circular room numbered LXXV, containing Spanish XVIIth. century pictures, and enters Hall LXXV, which is devoted to Flemish art of the XVIIth. century: Rubens, Quellyn, Cossiers, Jordaens, Cornelis de Vos, Gowi, Symons, Borkens and Jan Eyck.

HALL LXVIII. CORRIDOR

Here are a number of pictures by Luis de Morales, Juan de Juanes and Navarrete, Spanish painters of the XVIth. century, and Carducho, Pareja, Orrente, Arias, Valdés Leal, Palomino, Castillo, Donoso and others.

The small picture, *The Baptism of Christ* by Navarrete (the Dumb), was the means of introducing the artist's application for employment to King Philip IInd. This finely coloured and finished work was originally in El Escorial, coming to the Prado from the Academia de San Fernando in 1827.

Amont the paintings on exhibition in this Hall, the following four are also worthy of note and praise: *The Adoration of the Shepherds*, by Pedro de Orrente, which has an attractively simple air and is the best of the works of Orrente to be found in the Prado; *The Coin of Caesar*, by the Madrid artist Antonio Arias, of excellent technique, signed and dated 1646; *The Vocation of St. Matthew*, an original by Juan de Pareja, the slave and disciple of Velázquez, also signed and dated 1661, and the large-scale composition *The Death of the Venerable Carthusian Odón de Novara*, the best known of the series of 54 works that Vincencio Carducho painted for the Carthusian Monastery of El Paular, on subjects relating to the life of St. Bruno and several Saints of his Order; this series of paintings was on exhibition in the Museo de la Trinidad, until the dissolution of this Institution.

HALL LXXIV

Two undistinguished works by Valdés Leal—a *St. Jerome* and a figure of a martyr—are on exhibition here, and there are two more on the second floor, to which we shall refer in due course.

In order to appreciate Valdés Leal's work it is necessary to visit Seville, and it is interesting to recall that this artist, in his day, was considered a serious rival to the great Murillo, of whom he was violently jealous.

His *St. Jerome* reveals attractive brush-work spoiled by faulty design. Both this and *The Martyr* were painted for the Seville Church of St. Isabel, and were looted by the French during the Napoleonic wars. *St. Jerome* came to the Prado from Agnew House in London, in 1936, and *The Martyr* from the Madrid antiquary Sánchez Villalba in the previous year.

Claudio Coello's *St. Domingo de Guzmán*, and *St. Rosa de*

Lima are good examples of the sober Spanish style of the XVIIth. century. They are believed to have been commissioned for a Madrid Church before entering the Museo de la Trinidad, from whence they came to the Prado.

The Immaculate Conception, by José Antolínez, signed and dated 1663, was bought by the Prado in 1931.

The *Scene from the Life of St. Francis,* attributed to Juan Martín Cabezalero (1633-1673) was painted for the Madrid Convent of St. Hermenegildo, and was one of the 50 Spanish pictures looted during the Napoleonic invasion. It reached the Prado from the Academia de San Fernando in 1911. Some critics assert that it is the work of Claudio Coello, while others attribute it to Carreño but, lacking decisive evidence, it is still officially listed as being by Cabezalero.

HALL LXXII

This Hall contains some interesting portraits, including a canvas by Sánchez Coello of King Philip IInd.'s two daughters, Isabel Clara and Catalina Micaela.

There are also portraits of Elizabeth of Valois; and of King Philip IIIrd. and Margaret of Austria, by Juan Pantoja, whose work we have already seen. The style is similar to that of Coello, and possesses the same preoccupation with the model's clothes, rather than his character, typical of all Spanish portrait painters before Velázquez.

Rodrigo de Villandrando's portraits of King Philip IVth. and his first Queen are similar in treatment, but inferior in quality, to those of Pantoja.

The collection of paintings of flowers, shown against a dark background, by Juan de Arellano and Bartolomé Pérez, hardly require special comment, beyond the recognition that they are faithful copies from nature.

HALLS C, CI AND CII

To one side of Hall LXIX, facing the Museum Restaurant, there is a staircase marked XCIX, leading to the three Halls opened in 1958 in the Basement of the building, that are illuminated with artificial lighting.

On the staircase hang small paintings by Teniers.

Hall C is devoted to the few examples of the work of English painters to be found in the Museo del Prado. There are twelve portraits on exhibition (portraiture being the form of art in which the English painters excelled) by Reynolds, Gainsborough, Romney, Hoppner, Lawrence, Gordon and three anonymous artists; there are, further, two landscapes of Andalusia, in oils, by David Roberts, the great water-colour artist of the XIXth. century, who travelled in Spain during the vogue of Romanticism.

The portrait of a clergyman, by Reynolds (acquired for the Museum in 1943); that of a lady wearing a hat, by Hoppner (a legacy to the Museum from Don Luis de Errazu in 1925); the portrait of a gentleman by Romney (left to the Museum in 1935 by the Duque de Arcos), and those painted by Gordon and Lawrence (the latter, a full-length portrait, being most attractive) are, in our judgment, the most distinguished among the small number of works of English painters contained in the Museum.

Halls CI and CII contain about fifty works, in the majority painted by Dutch artists of the XVIIth. century, which give us an impression of the rather artificial and dull manner of the Dutch art of the period.

In addition to five lifts there are three large staircases by which the visitor may reach the First Floor. These are situated on the northern and southern side of the building and also in the centre. Two of these stairways continue from the Ist. to the IInd. Floor. The IInd. Floor is divided into two separate groups of halls, one of which forms a north square and the other a south square, both possessing direct light. The two groups have no communication between them, and the visitor is obliged, therefore, after completing his tour of one group, to descend to the Ist. Floor, and then ascend again by the stairs leading to the other group.

We have selected first to visit the southern group and, ascending the stairs marked LXXIX, upon which there are some Italian and Flemish canvases, we first enter the red silk tapestried hall LXXX, which is devoted to Mengs.

HALL LXXX

Anthony Raphael Mengs, born in Aussig in Bohemia, holds a rather special position in XVIIIth. century Spanish art. He lived in Spain for almost 10 years, and exercised a powerful influence upon his contemporaries, even when they were, like Goya, his artistic superiors. Mengs was not a great artist, preferring to concentrate all his efforts upon the elaboration of the conventional artistic theories of the time, which favoured the coldly studious rather than the inspirational, but he enjoyed enormous prestige during his lifetime. Mengs' admirers such as José Nicolás de Azara, believed that he was destined to become a second Raphael, and his writings reveal that at one time he exercised something like an artistic dictatorship in Spain.

If we could not ourselves examine Mengs' work we should be obliged to accept the opinion of him expressed by his contemporaries, but the Prado contains no less than 22 of his canvases and, after viewing them, we are forced to the conclusion that these opinions greatly exaggerated his talent. Mengs' painting is cold and, as one critic puts, it, «somehow a little tired», and his canvases always appear artificial and overburdened, and lacking in the essential grace and simplicity of line that it to be found in the work of all really great artists. The faces in his portraits often look as though they were made of porcelain, and all have an unattractively varnished appearance. Similarly, his works on religious themes fail to provoke any kind of enthusiasm, even the most important of them—his *Adoration of the Shepherds*, painted in Rome in 1770—lacking any kind of sincerity.

Mengs' portraits reveal some ability, their faulty technique being at least partly offset by accurate drawing and a clever use of colour when depicting his model's clothing. On the occasions when he managed to refrain from extensive, last minute, retouching, he could produce harmonious portraits, such as the head and shoulders of Maria Luisa of Parma. This is numbered 2.568, and was bequeathed to the Prado by the Duke of Tarifa in 1934. Other good examples of Mengs' work are his portraits of King Charles IIIrd. and of Leopold, Gran Duke of Tuscany. His use of colour is well displayed in another of Maria Luisa of Parma numbered 2189, and also in those of María Josefa de Lorraine, Archduchess of Austria; Maria Carolina of Lorraine, Queen of Naples, and of María Luisa de Bourbon, Grand Duchess of Tuscany. In all these portraits the painting of the dresses is exquisitely done.

Two other outstanding canvases by Mengs are his self-portrait, and that of the Prince who was later to become King Charles IVth.

In this same hall, which is mainly devoted to Mengs, there is a portrait of Anna von Muralt by the woman painter Angelica Kauffmann (1741-1807). Again the artist's reputation seems far in excess of her merits, and this canvas provides a fair example of the rigid German painting of the late XVIIIth. century. There

is an attractive small portrait by the Italian artist Battoni, entitled
A Traveller in Italy which, although no masterpiece, is pleasing.

> We leave Mengs' hall by the passage with drawings, num-
> bered LXXXI, which opens into three halls on each side.
> Those on the left hand are numbered LXXXII, LXXXIII and
> LXXXIV in the plan of the building. Before entering the second
> of these there is a small unnumbered hall containing 27 paint-
> ings by Lucca Giordano. The halls on the right of the passage
> are LXXXV, LXXXVI and LXXXVII.

The vehement Neapolitan Lucca Giordano (1632-1705) was,
like Tiepolo, far more successful as a painter of frescos than of
pictures. Both required the freedom of large wall or ceiling surfaces
to achieve their effects, and, confined to the limits of a canvas, the
results give us no real idea of their capacity, and the work before
us reveals the superficiality of an artist unsuccessfully attempting
to adapt himself to a medium that is not his own. Most of Giordano's
oil-paintings lack either accurate drawing or attractive colouring,
and some are the merest sketches. One of these sketches is particularly effective, however, showing that the artist was better at
conveying figures in movement than when stationary; this is
entitled *The Defeat of Sisara*.

It is related that when he was very young Giordano's father,
anxious for present profits rather than future fame, used con-
tinually to be shouting, *Luca, fa presto—Hurry up, Lucca*—and
the phrase has stuck to him, even to this day, as a nickname and
also a commentary upon his style and methods.

Lucca Giordano spent 10 years at the Royal Court of Spain,
being summoned there by King Charles IInd. in May 1692. He
worked far too rapidly for it to be possible for him to give his
paintings their proper finish, though this is less apparent in
his decorative work which, seen from a distance, is ornamentally
effective. However, when reduced to the limits of oil-paintings,
such as are on view here, he betrays himself as an unworthy
successor to Velázquez and Murillo.

HALL LXXXII

The contents of this hall were presented to the Prado under
the Will of Don Ramón de Errazu in 1904. They consist of nine

pictures by Raimundo de Madrazo, nine by Mariano Fortuny—six oils and three water-colours—; five by the landscape painter Martín Rico, and one each by the French artists Meissonier and Paul Baudry.

We have always held the opinion that the Prado should exhibit nothing of a later date than the works of Goya, believing that the correct place for all such works is in one of Madrid's Modern Art Galleries, the Museo Romántico of the Museo Nacional de Arte Moderno.

An objection to the Errazu Legacy, which is perhaps even more serious than that of not belonging to the historic tradition of the vast majority of the Prado's exhibits, is the fact that the pictures of which it is composed are frankly mediocre. An Art Gallery of the category of the Prado gains nothing by exhibiting the *Portrait of Queen María Cristina of Hapsburg* by Raimundo de Madrazo, or that of the Marchioness of Manzanedo by Meissonier, nor yet from the copy of Velázquez's head by Menipo; the small landscapes by Martín Rico; several of Fortuny's water-colours, and many others.

The best among the 25 pictures making up the Errazu Legacy are, in our view, the small nude study by Fortuny entitled *Women on the Sea Shore*, and Raimundo de Madrazo's portrait of the model Aline Masson wearing a white mantilla. The female nude by Madrazo, which is called *After the Bath*, strikes us as being inferior to *The Wave* by Baudry.

HALL LXXXIII

In this Hall are to be seen slightly more than thirty paintings by Spanish artists of the XVIIth. century. The works on display are by Alonso Cano, Murillo, Claudio Coello, Carreño, Francisco Rizi, Escalante, Collantes, Arias, Gilarte, Mazo, Esteban March, Juan de Toledo, Miguel Jacinto Meléndez, and others of lesser importance.

Among the works shown here, *Christ on the Cross* by Alonso Cano is, in our opinion, the most outstanding and valuable, both for its expressiveness and plastic qualities, which present an admirable example of the baroque treatment of this subject. (This painting, by the way, is not registered in the catalogue of the Museum.)

Also worthy of mention are two portraits, one of an Artillery General, painted by Rizi, and that of Father Cabanillas which, though originally attributed to Murillo, is now held to be by Claudio Coello. The head of the first of these two portraits is full of character.

Very interesting are two sketches by Meléndez, one representing *St. Augustin conjuring the plague of locusts,* and the other *The Burial of the Count of Orgaz* (this subject, as is known, having been immortalized by El Greco). These are beautifully finished sketches, in the baroque style, displaying an excellent technique.

HALL LXXXIV

Several artists of the XVIIIth. century—the Italians Antonio Joli, Giovanni Domenico Tiépolo, Canaletto, Panini and Amiconi, and the Spaniards Luis Paret, Francisco and Ramón Bayeu, Mariano Maella and the excellent still-life painter, Menéndez—are on exhibit in this Hall.

Joli is represented by two paintings of *The Embarkment of Carlos III in Naples;* Paret by two studies of flower-vases and two large compositions, evidently inferior to his charming small chamber paintings to be seen on the Main floor of the Museum. The Museum has on display four of the eight scenes from the Passion of our Lord painted by Tiepolo for the Madrid Church of San Felipe Neri (we have already seen the remainder of this series on the Main floor). The Bayeu brothers and Maella are represented by some oil paintings devoid of importance.

The *Views of Venice* catalogued under the name of the famous Giovanni Antonio Canal, known as *Canaletto,* are not authenticated. They were left to the Museum in 1930 by Don Xavier Laffite. However, the careful treatment and harmonious colouring are typical of his artist.

HALLS LXXXV, LXXXVI AND LXXXVII

These three Halls display, in the majority, paintings by Italian artists of the baroque period. In the Central Hall—which is the largest—there are 17 large compositions, revealing an art that is painstaking rather than inspired and, though already tainted with decadence, still contains great pictoric force and is executed with an admirable technique.

In the first place, we would give just praise to the five canvases by the Neapolitan Mássimo Stanzione that adorn this Hall: the *Sacrifice to Bacchus,* which is signed, and the four that make up a series on the life of St. John the Baptist, representing respectively, the birth of the Saint, the leave-taking from his parents, the preaching in the desert and the decapitation. These beautiful works have belonged to the Royal collections of Spain since the XVIIth. century. The subjects, so often treated by artists of the Renaissance period, are lent a certain grandeur by the brush of this artist.

Another two paintings on the *Birth of the Baptist* are to be seen in this Hall; one by Andrea Sacchi and one by Artemisia Gentileschi, the latter being signed. The critic Longhi considers it to be «the best achieved study of an interior in the whole of XVIIth. century Italian painting».

There are three works by Andrea Vaccaro on display here. The Museum has other works by the same artist on show in other Halls. Vaccaro is, without doubt, one of the most successful followers of the style of our artist Ribera, as may be appreciated here.

Moses rescued from the waters of the Nile, by Orazio Gentileschi, is a magnificent example of decorative painting, with its clear colouring and sumptuous figures. It is believed to have been commissioned by King Philip IVth.

There is not much worthy of note for the visitor in Hall LXXXV.

The Annunciation, by Daniel de Volterra, is of great interest for the exquisite distinction of its lines, so typical of the Florentine school.

Several paintings by the Bassano family to be seen here are

not comparable with the highly valuable ones we have already seen on the Main floor.

In Hall LXXXVII the most outstanding works are, in our opinion, the delightful *Virgin and Child* by Sassoferrato, a charming and tender version of this gentle subject, *Veronica*, by Strozzi and *The Assumption* by Anibal Carracci.

NORTHERN WING OF THE SECOND FLOOR

On the stairway connecting the Ist. Floor with the northern wing of the IInd. Floor the following work is to be seen: *Auto de Fe*, by Francisco Rizi.

Rizi's large panel, crowded with figures, has more historical than artistic value. It is signed and dated 1683, and records different aspects of the sentences carried out by the Inquisition in the Plaza Mayor of Madrid, in the presence of King Charles IInd. on June 30th. 1680.

Don Pedro de Madrazo, author of *Detailed Catalogue of the Prado*, devotes considerable attention to this picture. However, it is so dark as to be difficult to examine effectively.

HALLS LXXXIX, XC AND XCI

These three Halls are devoted to Flemish painting of the XVIIth. century.

In the first are to be seen paintings of hunting scenes and birds by Frans Snyders, Jan Fyt and Van Kessel; there are also landscapes and still-life studies by several artists, and a few compositions by Jan Brueghel de Velours.

Hall XCI contains, also, some charming rural scenes by the latter artist, such as that entitled *Country Wedding*, which pleases the beholder with its atmosphere of innocent gaiety and its attractive colouring.

Worthy of mention in Hall XC are the large, opulent still-life paintings by Snyders, Peter Boel and Adriaen Van Utrecht, undeniable masters in this type of painting. Among those by Van

Utrecht, the most remarkable are those entitled *Filopemenes discovered* and *A larder*, in which still-life objects acquire a highly sensuous quality.

The works representing the art of Peter Boel are equally excellent.

Poor in colouring, though possessing a sure draughtsmanship and fine composition, are the two paintings by Theodor Rombouts, *Card Players* and *The itinerant dentist*.

HALLS XCII, XCIII, XCIV, XCV AND XCVI

These five halls contain the pictures bequeathed to the Prado 34 years ago by Don Pedro Fernández Durán—«in memory of my father and mother, Don Miguel Fernández Durán and Doña Paula Bernaldo de Quirós, Marquesses of Perales and Tolosa»— to quote a plaque displayed here.

The legacy consisted of 80 pictures, mostly by non-Spanish artists, and a number of drawings, miniatures, arms, tapestries, sculptures, etc. The entire legacy is not on exhibition owing to lack of space, and only 50 out a collection of 3.000 drawings are to be seen here. These halls were inaugurated on June 18th, 1931, but the pictures were not hung until the conclusion of the 1942 catalogue. Among the pictures are works by Goya, Van der Weyden, Morales and Herrera (the Elder), and the largest individual representation is the twelve by the Flemish painter Franck (the Younger). Perhaps the most valuable part of the legacy consists of the five canvases by Goya, which are his *Portrait of General Ricardos*, *The Colossus*, *Blind Man's Buff*, *The Drunken Builder*, and *The Hermitage of St. Isidro*.

Other painters, whose work is represented in the Durán legacy, are the Spaniards, Orrente, Juan de Toledo, Carnicero and Ferro; the Italians, Giordano, Maratti, Amiconi and Caracciolo; the Flemish, Coffermans, Neefs (the Elder), Joris van Son, Frans Ikens, Van Kessel (the Elder), Teniers and Brouwer; the Dutch, Heda, Pieter Claeszon and Wouvermann; the French, Pillement, Oudry and Boullogne, and the German Vollardt.

Some of these painters were not represented in the Prado until the Durán legacy was made.

HALL XCVII

This Hall is devoted to French painting.

It is well-known that the Museum possesses few notable examples of this School. The best have already been seen on our visit to the Main floor.

Poussin, Beaubrun, Jouvenet, Drouais, Dorigny, Houasse, Coypel, Claude de Lorraine, Pillement, Gobert and Valentin are represented in this Hall.

Outstanding are the two mythological compositions by Michel Ange Houasse, a painter who worked in Spain at the service of Philip Vth. These two works were painted in Madrid; the one entitled *Bacchanal* in 1719; the *Sacrifice to Bacchus*, in 1720. Both compositions are harmoniously conceived; and since they were painted at a time that was already academic, the influence of the Academic style is evident in both.

Also worthy of note in this Hall are the works of Michel Dorigny and Jean Baptiste Jouvenet, the former with his decorative composition *The Triumph of Prudence*, and the latter with the beautiful sketch on a religious theme, *The Magnificat*.

HALL XCVIII

This contains portraits by Spanish artists, nearly all belonging to the XIXth. century. There are originals by Vicente and Bernardo López, José, Federico, Luis and Raimundo de Madrazo, Esquivel, Gutiérrez de la Vega, Zacarías González Velázquez, Fernández Cruzado and Luis Ferrant.

Among these works is exhibited a head and shoulders portrait of Mrs. Lolita Muth, by Ignacio Zuloaga, which became the property of the Museum in 1954, being legacy from the sitter; naturally, in view of Zuloaga's peculiar style, this portrait is not in harmony with the other paintings exhibited in the Hall, which are all imbued with a delicate Romantic air.

Federico de Madrazo, the best portraitist of his period, who painted the beauties of his time in masterly manner, has on exhibit here a beautiful likeness of the Condesa de Vilches, that betrays the influence of his master, Ingres. This portrait is rather ornate and pompous, but not devoid of distinction and charm, and is, furthermore, exquisitely painted. It was executed in 1853, and left to the Museum in 1944 by the sitter's son, the second Conde de Vilches.

The portraits of the Girona couple, dated 1856, and left to the Museum in 1941 by the Conde de Eleta, the son of the sitters, is a fine example of the art of Federico de Madrazo at its soberest and most admirable.

S C U L P T U R E

We have omitted reference of sculpture until now in order not to interfere with the main object of this book, which is a study of the paintings to be seen in the Prado.

However, as long ago as 1908, Don Eduardo Barrón catalogued no less than 400 examples of sculpture here and, since then, the number has been increased. But, although some of these are of real artistic value, they are frequently regarded as little more than an ornament to halls and galleries visited in order to see the pictures.

There are very few on the Second Floor, but there are some fine examples of sculpture in the Central Gallery, and the best are on the Ground Floor, where there are two halls devoted exclusively to them. The larger of these—Hall LVIII—contains no less than 800 statues, there being a special catalogue of its contents by Don Elías Tormo, entitled *The Hall of the Muses*.

In Hall LXXI there are twelve works exhibited in niches, including the famous pre-Christian *Lady of Elche*, and the three examples of Ancient Greek and Sumerio-Acadian art bequeathed to the Prado in 1943 by the Mexican, Don Mario de Zayas.

The bust of an Iberian priestess, known as *The Lady of Elche* came to the Prado in 1941 from the Louvre in Paris, where it had been since the beginning of the century. It is an important example of Iberian sculpture produced about 500 B. C., and was discovered on August 4th., 1897, in Alcudia, near Elche, by the French Archaeologist Pierre Paris. It was sold by the owner of the land on which it was discovered to Pierre Paris who presented it to the Louvre. It is made of calcareous stone with a faint trace of colouring, which suggests that it may have been the work of a Greek artist.

Nearly all the sculpture contained in the Prado came from the Royal Collection, and may be divided into two groups: the Graeco Roman, and the work of the XVIth. to XIXth. centuries. There are no examples of mediaeval sculpture. As is inevitable in such a collection, there are a number of pieces of unknown origin. Many pieces were part of the collections made by King Philip Vth. and his wife, Elizabeth Farnesio—this remarkable Queen bringing with her from Rome a quantity of statuary that had formerly been the property of Queen Christina of Sweden. There are additionally the pieces collected by the Emperor Charles Vth., and his son King Philip IInd. and also the gifts sent to Charles Vth. by Pope Paul IInd., and to Philip IInd. by Cardinal Montepulciano in 1561. Thirty Roman busts were presented to King Charles IVth, by the diplomat Don José Nicolás de Azara, who had purchased them in Italy. Lastly, there are a few pieces from the collection bought by Velázquez, when in Italy, at the orders of King Philip IVth.

Writing of the sculpture to be seen in the Prado, Camon says, «The greater part belongs to the Graeco-Roman period—a term which is admittedly inexact, but which cannot be avoided owing to the impossibility of separating the two overlapping civilizations. Many are, for example, Roman copies from Greek originals but, either directly or indirectly, Hellenic art is fairly represented here. The earliest examples are the representations of Apollo, which form part of the Zayas Legacy; then comes Aristogiton's head from the famous *Tyrannicides* group owned by the Naples Museum, which belongs to the early Vth. century B. C. The classic period of Greek sculpture is splendidly represented by a statue of the Diadumeno, inspired by that of Policleto.

There are more abundant traces of Phidias than of Praxiteles —his sensual and graceful style being immediately apparent—and there are a few examples of the passionate art of Scopa.

The series of busts are of the first importance, including the Greek—or Roman copies of the Greek originals—of Homer, Plato and Aristotle. The purely Roman ones are of Augustus, Lucio Vero and Caracalla, besides two splendid representations of Antinoo.»

Among the classical marble statues there are some striking examples of Phidias' School, notably the head of an Athenian horse, and a male torso, in Hall LXXI, this latter forming part of the Zayas Legacy.

Belonging to the Hellenic period *The Venus 'of the Shell* and *Hipnos* are of special value, while the Praxiteles School claims the so-called *Group of St. Ildephonsus* (perhaps representing Castor and Pollux) and also the *Faun and Kid, The Venus of the Dolphin* and *Aphrodite* bequeathed by Zayas.

Among the statues belonging to the late Renaissance period mention must be made of the Italians Leone and Pompeo Leoni, who left some admirable bronzes in Spain.

The Prado also contains the statue of the *Emperor Charles Vth.* in the Rotunda, and the armed figure of King Philip IInd. in Hall XXI.

THE DAUPHIN'S TREASURE

HALL LXXIII (GROUND FLOOR)

This famous treasure is composed of a number of fine jewelled chalices, inherited by King Philip Vth. of Spain from his father, the Dauphin. The Dauphin, as the eldest son, was heir presumptive to King Louis XIVth. of France, but pre-deceased «le roi Soleil» by three years.

It would appear that Philip Vth. received this inheritance without much interest, and ordered the whole collection to be sent to the Palace at La Granja, where it remained for several years. In 1734 it was catalogued, revealing that it consisted of 86 gems, set in gold, enamel or cameo, of which 71 are on exhibition here. To this number must be added the 49 pieces worked in rock crystal. All 120 are the work of Italian or French artists of the XVIth. and XVIIth. centuries.

Matilde López Serrano wrote of the Dauphin's Treasure, «It is only by recalling something of the history of France that we can understand how such treasure came into the possession of the House of Bourbon. The strong personal rivalry between the Emperor Charles Vth. of Spain and King Francis Ist. of France led to constant wars on Italian soil for the possession of Milan and the Kingdom of Naples, where the French monarch fell in love with the art, culture and luxury of the Renaissance, and employed a number of Italian artists to beautify his Court.

The Dauphin's Treasure was accumulated, therefore, by the last of the Valois and the early Bourbon Kings, a time when Italian craftsmanship was at its best. Formerly part of the Louvre collection it can only be compared with those to be seen in Vienna, Munich and Florence.

When, in 1776, King Charles IIIrd. of Spain founded the Royal Museum of Natural History he presented the entire collection to it but, during the period of the Napoleonic invasion, most of it was carried off to Paris, from whence it was returned after the Battle of Waterloo in 1815. However, by then 12 pieces had disappeared, and many among the remainder had been seriously damaged.

They have been on exhibition in the Prado since 1839, largely due to the efforts of Don José de Madrazo, who appreciated their artistic worth and, in 1886, they were repaired by the goldsmith Pedro Zaldos. During the Civil War, in 1937, the collection was again sent abroad, but returned in 1939.

The gems themselves are of diverse kinds; agate, turquoise, jasper, jade and lapizlazuli. Most of the agates are white, yellow, or a faint purple shade, while the jaspers are nearly all of a deep green colour, which contrasts attractively with the softer green of the jade, and the blue of the lapizlazuli and turquoises. Nearly all are set in enamelled gold or silver-gilt. Some of the finest examples of the gold and silver-smith's art are decorated by diamonds, emeralds, rubies, garnets, turquoises and blister pearls.»

Eleven pieces of the Dauphin's Treasure were stolen from the Prado in 1918, the robbery being discovered in September. The missing objects were never recovered, and the incident led to the resignation of the then Director and Assistant Director of the Prado.

ALPHABETICAL INDEX

OF THE PRINCIPAL PAINTERS REPRESENTED IN THE PRADO,
WITH THE HALLS WHERE THEY MAY BE SEEN, AND THE PAGE
NUMBERS WHERE MENTION OF THEM IS MADE

AMBERGER, Christof.—German. Born between 1500 and 1510; died about 1562.—HALL LIX. (Page 236.)

ANGELICO, Fra (Guido di Pietro da Mugello).—Italian. Born in Vicchio di Mugello (Florence) in 1387; died in Rome in 1455.—HALL III. (Page 72.)

ANTOLINEZ, José.—Spanish. Born in Madrid in 1635; died in Madrid in 1675.—HALLS XXIX and LXXIV. (Pages 195 and 266.)

ARELLANO, Juan de.—Spanish. Born in Santorcaz (Madrid) in 1614; died in Madrid in 1676.—HALL LXXII (Page 266.)

ARGUIS, Master of.—Spanish. Unknown Aragonese painter of the mid 15th. century.—HALL L. (Page 227.)

BALDUNG, Hans.—German. Born in Weyersheim between 1476 and 1485; died in 1545.—HALL XLIV. (Page 65.)

BASSANO, Jacopo da Ponte.—Italian. Born in Bassano between 1510 and 1515; died in 1592.—HALLS X A and LXXXV. (Pages 105, 106 and 273.)

BAYEU, Francisco.—Spanish. Born in Zaragoza in 1734; died in Madrid in 1795.—HALLS XXXI and LXXXIV. (Pages 200 and 272.)

BELLINI, Giovanni.—Italian. Born in Venice or Padova, about 1430; died in Venice in 1516.—HALL IV. (Page 73.)

BENSON, Ambrosius.—Flemish. Born in Bruges; died in 1550.—HALL LIX. (Page 236.)

BERMEJO Bartolomé.—Spanish. Born in Córdoba, and painted between 1474 and 1495.—HALL XXIV. (Pages 68 and 69.)

BERRUGUETE, Pedro.—Spanish. Believed to have been born in Paredes de Nava (Palencia) about 1450; died about 1503.—HALLS XXIV, XLV and L. (Pages 67 and 68.)

BOSCH, Hieronymus Van Aeken.—Dutch. Born in Bois-le-Duc about 1450; died in 1516.—HALLS XLIII and XLIV. (Pages 46 to 48.)

BOTTICELLI, Sandro (Alessandro Filipepi).—Italian. Born in Florence in 1444 or 1445; died there in 1510. HALL III. (Pages 72 and 73.)

BOUTS, Thierry or Dieric.—Flemish. Born in Harlem about 1420; died in Louvain in 1475.—HALL XL. (Page 42.)

BRONZINO, IL (AGNOLO DI COSIMO ALLORI).—Italian. Born in Monticelli (near Florence) in 1503; died in Florence in 1572.—HALL V. (Page 75.)

BRUEGHEL, the Old, PEETER.—Flemish. Born probably in Brueghel (Dutch Brabante) about 1525; died in Brussels in 1569.—HALL XLIII. (Pages 45 and 46.)

BRUEGHEL DE VELOURS, JAN.—Flemish. Born in Brussels in 1568; died in Antwerp in 1625.—HALL LXVII. (Pages 263 and 264.)

CABEZALERO, JUAN MARTÍN.—Spanish. Born in Almadén (Ciudad Real) in 1633; died in Madrid in 1673.—HALL LXXIV (Page 266.)

CALLET, ANTOINE FRANÇOIS.—French. Born in Paris in 1741; died in Paris in 1825.—HALL XXXIII. (Page 201.)

CANALETTO, IL (GIOVANNI ANTONIO CANAL).—Italian. Born in Venice in 1697; died there in 1768.—HALL LXXXIV. (Page 272.)

CANO, ALONSO.—Spanish. Born in Granada in 1601; died there in 1667.— HALLS XXIX, LXIII and LXXXIII. (Pages 195, 258, 259 and 271.)

CARNICERO, ANTONIO.—Spanish. Born in Salamanca in 1748; died in Madrid in 1814.—HALL XXXI. (Page 200.)

CARREÑO DE MIRANDA, JUAN.—Spanish. Born in Avilés in 1614; died in Madrid in 1685.—HALLS XXIX, LXIII and LXIV. (Pages 196, 258 and 259.)

CASTILLO, ANTONIO DEL.—Spanish. Born in Córdoba in 1616 and died there in 1668.—HALL LXIII A. (Page 260.)

CATENA, IL (VINCENZO DI BIAGIO).—Italian. Believed to have been born in Venice about 1470 and died there in 1531.—HALL IV. (Page 73.)

CEREZO, MATEO.—Spanish. Born in Burgos about 1626; died in Madrid in 1666.—HALL XXIX. (Page 194.)

CLAESZON VAN REYMERSWAELE, MARINUS.—Dutch. Born in Zeeland towards the end of the 15th. century; died in 1567.—HALLS XLIV, LX and LX A. (Pages 237 and 238.)

COELLO, CLAUDIO.—Spanish. Born in 1642, in Madrid, where he died in 1693.—HALLS XXIX, LXIV, LXV and LXXIV. (Pages 194, 260 and 265.)

COLLANTES, FRANCISCO.—Spanish. Born in Madrid in 1599; died in 1656, probably in Madrid.—HALL LXV. (Page 263.)

CORREA DE VIVAR, JUAN.—Spanish. A Castilian. He worked about the middle of the 16th. century.—HALL XLIX. (Page 229.)

CORREGGIO, IL (ANTONIO ALLEGRI).—Italian. Born in Correggio in 1493; died there in 1534.—HALL V. (Page 75.)

CRANACH, the Old, LUCAS.—German. Born in Kronach in 1472; died at Weimar in 1553.—HALL XLIV. (Page 65.)

CRESPI, DANIELLE.—Italian. Born in Busto Arsizio about 1592; died in Milan in 1630.—HALL XXXVIII. (Page 205.)

DAVID, GERARD.—Flemish. Born in Oudewater between 1450 and 1460; died in Bruges in 1523. HALL XLII. (Pages 44 and 45.)

DOMENICHINO, IL (DOMENICO ZAMPIERI).—Italian. Born in Bologna in 1591; died in Naples in 1641.—Second Floor.

DÜRER, ALBRECHT.—German. Born in Nuremberg in 1471; died there in 1528.—HALL XLIV. (Pages 48 and 65.)

FLEMALLE, THE MASTER OF.—Flemish. Unknown painter of the first half of the 15th. century.—HALL XL. (Page 42.)

FORTUNY, MARIANO.—Spanish. Born in Reus in 1838; died in Rome in 1874. HALL LXXXII. (Page 271.)

FRANCES, MAESTRE NICOLÁS.—He worked in León before 1434; died in 1468.—HALL L. (Page 226.)

GADDI, TADDEO.—Italian. Born in Florence in 1300; died there in 1367.—HALL IV. (Page 73.)

GALLEGO, FERNANDO.—Spanish. He worked between 1466 and 1507.—HALL XXIV. (Page 69.)

GARCIA DE BENABARRE, PEDRO.—Spanish. Born probably in Benabarre (Huesca). He worked about the middle of the 15th. century.—HALL L. (Page 226.)

GIORDANO, LUCCA.—Italian. Born in 1632 in Naples, where he died in 1705.—Second Floor. (Page 270.)

GIORGIONE, IL (GIORGIO DE CASTELFRANCO).—Italian. Born in Castelfranco Veneto about 1474; died in Venice in 1510.—HALL VI. (Page 76.)

GOSSAERT, JAN (OR «JAN DE MABUSE»).—Flemish. Born in Maubege about 1478; died between 1533 and 1536, probably in Middelbourg.—HALL XL. (Page 41.)

GOYA, FRANCISCO.—Spanish. Born in Fuendetodos (Zaragoza) in 1746; died in Bordeaux in 1828.—HALLS XXXII, LIII, LIV, LV, LVI, LVII, LV A, LVI A and LVII A. (Pages 196 to 199, 231 to 236.)

GRECO, EL (DOMENIKOS THEOTOKOPOULOS).—A Greek who lived in Spain. Born in Crete in 1541; died in Toledo in 1614.—HALLS X, XI and XXX. (Pages 107 to 112.)

GREUZE, JEAN BAPTISTE.—French. Born in Tournus in 1725; died in Paris in 1801.—Second Floor.

GUERCINO, IL (FRANCISCO GIOVANNI BARBIERI).—Italian. Born in Cento in 1591; died in Bologna in 1665.—HALL XXXVII. (Page 205.)

HERRERA, *the Old*, FRANCISCO DE.—Spanish. Born in Sevilla about 1576; died in Madrid in 1656.—HALL LXIV. (Page 260.)

HERRERA, *the Younger*, FRANCISCO DE.—Spanish. Born in Sevilla in 1622; died in Madrid in 1685.—HALL XXIX. (Page 195.)

HOBBEMA, MEINDERT.—Dutch. Born in Amsterdam in 1638; died there in 1709.—HALL XXIII. (Page 174.)

HOUASSE, MICHEL-ANGE.—French. Born in Paris in 1680; died in Arpajon in 1730.—HALLS XXXIV and XCVII. (Page 276.)

HUGUET, JAIME.—Spanish. He painted in Barcelona between 1448 and 1487. HALL L. (Page 227.)

JORDAENS, JACOB.—Flemish. Born in 1593 in Antwerp where he died in 1678.—HALL XVII A. (Pages 170 and 171.)

JUANES, JUAN DE (VICENTE JUAN MASIP).—Spanish. Born probably in Fuente de la Higuera (Valencia) about 1523; died in Bocairente in 1579.—HALLS XLIX and LXVIII. (Pages 229 and 230.)

KAUFFMANN, ANGELICA.—German. Born in Chur (Switzerland) in 1741; died in Rome in 1807.—HALL LXXX. (Page 269.)

LEONARDO, JUSEPE.—Spanish. Born in Calatayud about 1605; died in Zaragoza in 1656.—HALLS I and LXIV. (Pages 39 and 260.)

LOPEZ, VICENTE.—Spanish. Born in Valencia in 1772; died in Madrid in 1850.—HALLS XXXIX and XXXI. (Pages 206 and 207.)

LORRAINE, CLAUDE DE (CLAUDE GELLEÉ).—French. Born in a castle near Mirecourt in 1600; died in Rome in 1682.—HALLS XXXV, XXXVI and XCVII. (Pages 204 and 276.)

LOTTO, LORENZO.—Italian. Born in Venice in 1480; died in Loreto in 1556.—HALL VI. (Page 76.)

LUINI, BERNARDINO.—Italian. Born in Luino (Lombardy) between 1480 and 1485; died in 1532.—HALL V. (Page 75.)

MACHUCA, PEDRO.—Spanish. Born in Toledo, towards the end of the 15th. century; died in Granada in 1550.—HALL XLIX. (Page 229.)

MADRAZO, FEDERICO DE.—Spanish. Born in Rome in 1815; died in Madrid in 1894.—HALL XCVIII. (Page 277.)

MADRAZO, RAIMUNDO DE.—Spanish. Born in Rome in 1841; died in Versailles in 1920.—HALLS LXXXII and XCVIII. (Pages 271 and 276.)

MAELLA, MARIANO SALVADOR.—Spanish. Born in Valencia in 1739; died in Madrid in 1819.—HALLS XXXI and LXXXIV. (Page 272.)

MAINO, FRAY JUAN BAUTISTA.—Spanish. Born in Pastrana in 1578; died in Madrid in 1649.—HALL XXV. (Page 130.)

MANTEGNA, ANDREA.—Italian. Born in Isola di Cartura (Padova) in 1431; died in Mantua in 1506.—HALL IV. (Pages 73 and 74.)

MARTINEZ DEL MAZO, JUAN BAUTISTA.—Spanish. Born probably in Beteta about 1620; died in Madrid in 1667.—HALL LXIV. (Pages 260 and 261.)

MASIP, VICENTE JUAN.—Spanish. Born about 1475 in Valencia; died between 1545 and 1550.—HALL XLIX. (Pages 227 and 228.)

MEISSONIER, JEAN LOUIS ERNEST.—French. Born in Lyons in 1815; died in Paris in 1891.—HALL LXXXII. (Page 271.)

MELENDEZ, LUIS EUGENIO.—Spanish. Born in Naples in 1716; died in Madrid in 1780.—HALL XXXI. (Page 200.)

MELOZZO DA FORLI.—Italian. Born in 1438, in Forli. where he died in 1494.—HALL IV. (Page 73.)

MEMLING, HANS.—Flemish. Born in Mömling about 1433; died in Bruges in 1494.—HALL XLI. (Page 44.)

MENGS, ANTHONY RAPHAEL.—German. Born in Aussig (Bohemia) in 1728; died in Rome in 1779.—HALL LXXX. (Pages 268 and 269.)

METSU, GABRIEL.—Dutch. Born in Leyden in 1629; died in Amsterdam i 1667.—HALL XXII. (Page 174.)

METSYS, QUENTIN.—Flemish. Born in Louvain in 1465 or 1466; died ii Antwerp in 1530.—HALL XL. (Page 41.)

MIGNARD, PIERRE.—French. Born in Troyes in 1612; died in Paris in 1693.—HALL XXXVI. (Page 204.)

MOOR, ANTHONY (ANTON VAN DASHORST).—Dutch. Born in Utrecht about 1520; died in Antwerp in 1576.—HALL LX. (Pages 237 and 238.)

MORALES, LUIS DE.—Spanish. Born about 1500, in Badajoz, where he died in 1586.—HALLS XLIX and LXVIII. (Page 228.)

MURILLO, BARTOLOMÉ ESTEBAN.—Spanish. Born in 1617, in Sevilla, where he died in 1682.—HALLS XXVIII, LXI and LXII. (Pages 175 to 193 and 238 to 240.)

NAVARRETE, JUAN FERNÁNDEZ («EL MUDO»).—Spanish. Born in Logroño about 1526; died in Toledo in 1579.—HALL LXVIII. (Page 265.)

NUÑEZ DE VILLAVICENCIO, PEDRO.—Spanish. Born in 1644, in Sevilla, where he died in 1700.—HALL XXIX. (Page 195.)

PALMA, the Old (JACOPO NIGRETI).—Italian. Born in Serina (Bergamo) about 1480; died in 1528.—HALL VII. (Page 76.)

PANTOJA DE LA CRUZ, JUAN.—Spanish. Born in Valladolid in 1553; died in Madrid in 1608.—HALLS XLIX and LXXII. (Pages 231 and 266.)

PAREJA, JUAN DE.—Spanish. Born in Sevilla about 1610; died in Madrid in 1670.—HALL LXVIII. (Page 265.)

PARET. LUIS.—Spanish. Born in 1746, in Madrid, where he died in 1799.—HALLS XXXIX and LXXXIV. (Pages 206 and 272.)

PARMIGIANINO, IL (GIROLAMO FRANCESCO MARIA MAZZOLA).—Italian. Born in Rome in 1503; died in 1540.—HALL V. (Page 75.)

PATINIR, JOACHIM.—Flemish. Born in Dinant about 1480; died in Antwerp in 1524.—HALL XLIII. (Page 45.)

PEREDA, ANTONIO DE.—Spanish. Born in Valladolid about 1608; died in Madrid in 1678.—HALL XXV. (Page 132.)

PEREZ, BARTOLOMÉ.—Spanish. Born in 1634, in Madrid, where he died in 1693.—HALL LXXII. (Page 266.)

PIOMBO, FRA SEBASTIANO DEL.—Italian. Born about 1485; died in Rome in 1547.—HALL V. (Page 75.)

PONTE, GIOVANNI DAL.—Italian. Born in Florence. He lived between 1376 and 1437.—HALL IV. (Page 73.)

POUSSIN, NICOLAS.—French. Born in Les Andelys (Normandy) in 1594; died in Rome in 1665.—HALLS XXXIV and XXXV. (Pages 203 and 204.)

RANC, JEAN.—French. Born in Montpellier in 1674; died in Madrid in 1735; Second Floor.

RAPHAEL (RAFFAELLO SANZIO OR DA URBINO).—Italian. Born in Urbino in 1483; died in Rome in 1520.—HALL II. (Pages 69 to 71.)

REMBRANDT, HARMENSZ VAN RYN.—Dutch. Born in Leyden in 1606; died in Amsterdam in 1669.—HALLS XXII and XXIII. (Page 174.)

RENI, GUIDO.—Italian. Born in Calvezzano in 1575; died in 1642.—HALL XXXVII. (Page 205.)

REYNOLDS, SIR JOSHUA.—English. Born in Plympton-Earl's (Devonshire) in 1723; died in London in 1792.—HALL C. (Page 267.)

RIBALTA, FRANCISCO.—Spanish. Born in Solsona about 1560; died in Valencia in 1628.—HALLS XXV and LXV. (Pages 129, 130 and 262.)

RIBERA. JOSÉ DE («EL ESPAÑOLETO»).—Spanish. Born in Játiva in 1591; died in Naples in 1652.—HALLS XXVI, XLV, LXI A and LXII A. (Pages 132 to 134, 175, 238, 257 and 258.)

RICO, MARTÍN.—Spanish. Born in Madrid in 1833; died in Venice in 1908.—HALL LXXXII. (Page 271.)

RIGAUD, HYACINTHE.—French. Born in Perpignan in 1659; died in Paris in 1743.—HALL XXXV. (Page 203.)

RIZI, FRANCISCO.—Spanish. Born in Madrid in 1608; died in El Escorial in 1685.—HALL LXIV. (Pages 261 and 274.)

RIZI, FRAY JUAN.—Spanish. Born in Madrid in 1600; died in Montecassino (Italy) in 1681.—HALLS XXVI and LXIII A. (Pages 132 and 260.)

ROMNEY, GEORGE.—English. Born in Dalton-le-Furness (Lancashire) in 1734; died in Kendal in 1802.—HALL C. (Page 267.)

RUBENS, PETER PAUL.—Flemish. Born in Siegen (Westfalia) in 1577; died in Antwerp in 1640.—HALLS XVI, XVII, XVIII, XVIII A, XIX, XX and LXXV. (Pages 166 to 168, 170 to 173.)

SANCHEZ COELLO, ALONSO.—Spanish. Born in Benifayó (Valencia) in 1531 or 1532; died in Madrid in 1588.—HALLS XLIX, LXVIII and LXXII. (Pages 230 and 266.)

SARTO, ANDREA DEL.—Italian. Born in 1486, in Florence, where he died in 1531.—HALL V. (Pages 74 and 75.)

VELAZQUEZ, Diego Rodríguez de Silva.—Spanish. Born in Sevilla in 1599; died in Madrid in 1660.—HALLS XII, XIII, XIV, XIV A and XV. (Pages 134 to 166.)

VERONESE, Il (Paolo Caliari).—Italian. Born in Verona, probably in 1528; died in Venice in 1588.—HALLS VII A and VIII A. (Pages 77 to 79 and 97.)

WATTEAU, Jean Antoine.—French. Born in Valenciennes in 1684; died in Nogent-sur-Marne in 1721.—HALL XXXV. (Page 204.)

YAÑEZ DE LA ALMEDINA, Fernando.—Spanish. Born probably in La Almedina (Ciudad Real), and worked during the first half of the XVIth. century.—HALL XLIX. (Page 229.)

ZURBARAN, Francisco de.—Spanish. Born in Fuente de Cantos (Badajoz) in 1598; died in Madrid in 1664.—HALLS XXV and LXV. (Pages 131, 240 and 257.)

A MAGNIFICENT BOOK EDITED BY THE
COMPAÑIA BIBLIOGRAFICA ESPAÑOLA, S. A.

MADRID

LA VIDA Y LA OBRA
DE VELAZQUEZ

BY

BERNARDINO DE PANTORBA

THIS BOOK IS THE MOST COMPLETE WORK ON THE
GREAT SPANISH PAINTER THAT HAS BEEN PUBLISHED
IN THE WORLD
IT CONTAINS REPRODUCTIONS OF ALL THE PAINTINGS
OF THE MASTER, AND A MOST EXTENSIVE CRITICAL
CATALOGUE OF ALL THE WORK OF VELAZQUEZ